MORAL RESPONSIBILITY AND ARTIFICIAL INTELLIGENCE

This book introduces a novel puzzle, the 'Lorry Driver Paradox', to advance our understanding of moral responsibility beyond current paradigms, to connect moral philosophy and legal scholarship in new ways, and to break new ground in the ethics of AI.

Part One introduces the Lorry Driver Paradox as a set of three individually plausible but jointly inconsistent claims. It then develops and defends the concept of strict moral answerability as the most effective solution, making it the central idea of the book, alongside an account of how 'taking responsibility' could amount to a new, hitherto neglected normative power and an exploration of the significance of apologies in our social practices.

Part Two extends this discussion to the context of artificial intelligence, proposing a major shift in how we currently think about responsibility and AI. It challenges the conventional notion of AI-generated 'responsibility gaps' and, instead, proposes the idea of 'responsibility abundance'. This reframing, it is argued, offers distinct theoretical, dialectical, and practical advantages.

Significant parts of these arguments draw on legal scholarship, particularly considerations about reverse burdens of proof in criminal law and the waiving of state immunity in public international law. On these grounds, the book also pursues the methodological idea of a 'legal lead', that is, the idea that we can advance our understanding of moral responsibility by investigating (selected aspects of) legal responsibility, and not just the other way around.

Volume 17 in the series Law and Practical Reason

Law and Practical Reason

The intention of this series is that it should encompass monographs and collections of essays that address the fundamental issues in legal philosophy. The foci are conceptual and normative in character, not empirical. Studies addressing the idea of law as a species of practical reason are especially welcome. Recognizing that there is no occasion to sharply distinguish analytic and systematic work in the field from historico-critical research, the editors also welcome studies in the history of legal philosophy. Contributions to the series, inevitably crossing disciplinary lines, will be of interest to students and professionals in moral, political, and legal philosophy.

Recent titles in the series

Volume 8: Private Law and the Value of Choice
Emmanuel Voyiakis

Volume 9: Freedom and Force: Essays on Kant's Legal Philosophy
Edited by *Sari Kisilevsky and Martin J Stone*

Volume 10: The Nature and Value of Vagueness in the Law
Hrafn Asgeirsson

Volume 11: Law's Humility: Enlarging the Scope of Jurisprudential Disagreement
Triantafyllos Gkouvas

Volume 12: Rightful Relations with Distant Strangers: Kant, the EU, and the Wider World
Aravind Ganesh

Volume 13: The Making of Constitutional Democracy: From Creation to Application of Law
Paolo Sandro

Volume 14: New Essays on the Nature of Legal Reasoning
Edited by Mark McBride and James Penner

Volume 15: New Essays on the Fish-Dworkin Debate
Edited by Thomas Bustamante and Margaret Martin

Volume 16: A Dynamic Approach to Hans Kelsen's General Theory of Norms
Monika Zalewska

Volume 17: Moral Responsibility and Artificial Intelligence
Maximilian Kiener

Moral Responsibility and Artificial Intelligence

Maximilian Kiener

• HART •
OXFORD • LONDON • NEW YORK • NEW DELHI • SYDNEY

HART PUBLISHING

Bloomsbury Publishing Plc

Kemp House, Chawley Park, Cumnor Hill, Oxford, OX2 9PH, UK

1385 Broadway, New York, NY 10018, USA

Bloomsbury Publishing Ireland Limited, 29 Earlsfort Terrace, Dublin 2, D02 AY28, Ireland

HART PUBLISHING, the Hart/Stag logo, BLOOMSBURY and the Diana logo are trademarks of Bloomsbury Publishing Plc

First published in Great Britain 2025

A catalogue record for this book is available from the British Library.

A catalogue record for this book is available from the Library of Congress.

ISBN: HB: 978-1-50995-684-5
ePDF: 978-1-50995-686-9
ePub: 978-1-50995-685-2

Typeset by Compuscript Ltd, Shannon

For product safety related questions contact productsafety@bloomsbury.com

To find out more about our authors and books visit www.hartpublishing.co.uk. Here you will find extracts, author information, details of forthcoming events and the option to sign up for our newsletters.

Acknowledgements

THIS WORK WAS generously supported by the European Research Council under the European Union's Horizon 2020 research and innovation programme (Project ID: 789270) and the Leverhulme Trust through an Early Career Fellowship (ECF-2021-176). I am deeply grateful for this crucial funding, which allowed the research to be carried out.

I would also like to extend my sincere thanks to numerous colleagues who provided invaluable feedback on prior versions of this manuscript or parts of it. In particular, I am grateful to: Hannah Altehenger, Mireia Artigot Golobardes, Holger Baumann, Jonas Bozenhard, Gunnar Björnsson, Matthew Braham, Susanne Burri, Ben Colburn, Vincent Conitzer, Simon-Pierre Chevarie-Cossette, Mark Coeckelbergh, Roger Crisp Michael Da Silva, Gabriel de Marco, Matthew Dennis, Katrin Devolder, Thomas Douglas, Antony Duff, Timothy Endicott, David Enoch, Thomas Grote, Tim Henning, Rafaela Hillerbrand, Johannes Himmelreich, John Hyman, Anneli Jeffersonm, Simon Kirchin, Sebastian Köhler, Peter Königs, Thomas Krödel, Hélène Landemore, Andrew Lloyd, Erasmus Mayr, Elinor Mason, Leonhard Menges, Crescente Molina, Vincent Müller, Peter Niesen, Sven Nyholm, Yuuki Ohta, Dennis Patterson, Carina Prunkl, Lubomira Radoilska, Alexander Sarch, Peter Schaber, Michael Schefczyk, Thomas Schmidt, David Shoemaker, Judith Simon, Victor Tadros, John Tasioulas, Valentin Weber, Dominic Wilkinson, Susan Wolf, Shannon Vallor, Marcel van Ackeren, Tillmann Vierkant, Ulla Wessels, Sebastian Weydner-Volkmann, Karen Yeung, and John Zerilli. Their thoughtful insights and comments were instrumental in refining the ideas and arguments presented here. I am also grateful to the audiences at the following institutions and conferences, where I had the opportunity to present and discuss my work: Bonn University, Bratislava University, Hamburg University, LMU Munich, the London Institute of Philosophy, Paris Polytechnique, TU Eindhoven, the University of Edinburgh, the University of Glasgow, the University of Kent, the University of Neuchâtel, the University of Oldenburg, the University of Oxford, the University of Salzburg, the University of Southampton, the University of St Andrews, the University of Tübingen and the University of Zurich. Additionally, I extend my thanks to the attendees of the following conferences: the 2024 DKPhil Münster, the 2022 GAP11 at Humboldt University Berlin, the 2022 Joint Session, the 2022 Society for Applied Philosophy Conference and the 2021 CEPE IACAP Conference.

I also extend my heartfelt thanks to the team at Hart, especially George Pavlakos, Kate Whetter and Verity Stuart, for their excellent support throughout the publication process.

I thank the journals *Ethics, Ethical Theory and Moral Practice* and *The Journal of Applied Philosophy* for publishing parts of this book as journal articles and permitting their re-use as chapters in this book. Most of all, I am very grateful to my family, whose love and encouragement have made everything possible.

Contents

Introduction

BERNARD WILLIAMS FAMOUSLY explored the case of a 'lorry driver who, through no fault of his, runs over a child' (Williams 1981, 28). Williams used this scenario to investigate the rationality of a moral emotion he called *agent-regret*, a feeling of deep sadness over one's involvement in an outcome which one could not meaningfully control and is not morally culpable for. In this book, I shall use Williams's example for another purpose, namely, to introduce a novel challenge to our understanding of responsibility, which I call the *Lorry Driver Paradox*. This paradox consists of three individually plausible but jointly inconsistent claims. I state the paradox briefly here and shall elaborate on it in chapter one: (1) the faultless driver is not genuinely morally responsible for the child's death; (2) *Apology Principle*: one ought to apologise for something only if one is morally responsible for it; (3) the driver ought to apologise for the child's death.

In addressing the *Lorry Driver Paradox*, I pursue three main objectives. First, I shall challenge two paradigms in the philosophy of responsibility that have mostly transcended the field's otherwise pervasive controversy. The first paradigm, which I shall refer to as the *Reflection View*, holds that moral *answerability*, understood as a form of moral responsibility, requires an action to reflect the agent's judgement. Prominent scholars, such as David Shoemaker, Angela Smith and TM Scanlon, share this view. For instance, Shoemaker says that '[o]ne is an answerable agent … in virtue of one's quality of judgment' (Shoemaker 2015, 82) and Smith claims that '[i]n order for an agent to be answerable for something, … the thing in question must in some way reflect her own judgment or assessment of reasons' (Angela Smith 2015, 103). The second paradigm, which I shall call *Historicism*, posits that responsibility is grounded solely in the facts about how an action or outcome came about, and cannot be altered after the fact. Elinor Mason summarises this view: 'Responsibility cannot be taken after the fact, because responsibility is determined by the history of the act, and that is essential to the concept of responsibility' (Mason 2023, 364). There is a tight connection between the *Reflection View* and *Historicism*. If answerability, as a form of moral responsibility, requires reflection of judgement, and if, as seems plausible, reflection of judgement can only come about through a certain causal-agential history of an outcome, then Historicism must be true as well. One cannot forge a reflection of judgement after the fact. The central idea of this book, which is the concept of *strict* moral answerability, solves the *Lorry Driver Paradox* by countering the *Reflection View*, and thereby also prepares the grounds for a normative power of taking responsibility which then challenges *Historicism*. Strict moral answerability means, roughly, a form of responsibility without any requirement of fault or special connection to the agent's judgement. Strict moral answerability converges on a common philosophical definition of responsibility as answerability, but it proposes a radically different, legally inspired, sufficient condition. The normative power of taking responsibility, on the other hand, means the ability to make oneself responsible at will or by declaration, even after the fact, and this idea is conceived in analogy to other normative powers, such as consenting or promising.

The second objective of this book is to uncover new connections between philosophical and legal perspectives on responsibility. In particular, I shall explore how the criminal law on reverse burdens of proof supports the concept of strict answerability, and how international public law on the topic of waiving state immunity supports the idea of a normative power of taking responsibility. I argue that these aspects are not legal peculiarities but rather that they hold fundamental moral significance, such that we need to incorporate them into our frameworks of moral responsibility too, where they are currently lacking. This will lead me to the beginning of a potentially much larger hypothesis, namely that of the *Legal Lead*. The *Legal Lead* is the methodological claim that we can advance our understanding of moral responsibility by investigating (selected aspects of) legal responsibility, and not just the other way around.

Finally, and this is my third objective, I aim to show that the *Lorry Driver Paradox* not only helps us investigate the fundamentals of legal and moral responsibility, but also brings to light pressing questions in the context of artificial intelligence (AI). I argue that there is a challenge in the domain of AI, parallel to the *Lorry Driver Paradox*, which I call the *Autonomous AI Conundrum*. This conundrum arises in situations where generally beneficial, yet difficult-to-control and opaque AI systems cause harm – for instance, when an autonomous vehicle runs over a pedestrian or a surgical robot paralyses a patient. These AI cases, I claim, bear significant resemblance to Williams's original lorry driver scenario, allowing us to apply insights from traditional moral responsibility debates to the emerging challenges of AI. This parallel is particularly relevant to the discussion of so-called 'responsibility gaps' – instances where, arguably, no individual can be held morally responsible for harm caused by AI. In response, I shall argue that a model of strict moral answerability, combined with the normative power of taking responsibility, can help bridge these gaps. This leads to a novel proposal, which I term the *ABC of Responsible AI*, offering a framework for addressing responsibility in the age of autonomous systems.

Overall, then, this book introduces a novel puzzle, the *Lorry Driver Paradox*, in order to advance our understanding of moral responsibility beyond current paradigms, to connect moral philosophy and legal scholarship in new ways, and to break new ground in the ethics of AI. Part I introduces the *Lorry Driver Paradox* and defends strict moral answerability as the best way to solve it, making it the central idea of this book. In Part II, this discussion is extended to the context of artificial intelligence, applying and further developing the insights from the initial analysis to the emerging challenges posed by AI systems.

Part I

Moral Responsibility

1

*The Lorry Driver Paradox**

WILLIAMS DESCRIBED THE case of a 'lorry driver who, through no fault of his, runs over a child' (Williams 1981, 28). The driver is without fault and, as many have argued, not morally responsible because he could not possibly have foreseen the accident, was unable to prevent it when it happened, and did not display any other flaw in his conduct. But Williams says that, unlike bystanders who are equally faultless, the driver is likely to feel 'agent-regret' (Williams 1981, 27), ie the wish, accompanied by sadness, that things connected to his agency had turned out differently. Others may try to comfort the driver, remind him that it was not his fault, and help him to overcome his emotional distress. Yet, Williams insists, the driver's feeling of agent-regret is entirely appropriate and may make the driver perform 'actions … [that] have some reparative significance other than compensation' (Williams 1981, 29). In fact, it would seem morally appalling if the driver did not feel any agent-regret at all and simply shrugged off the accident. At a minimum, according to Susan Wolf, the driver ought to 'apologize' (Wolf 2001, 13).

However, once we accept this description of Williams's case (alongside a widely accepted *Apology Principle)*, we face the following individually plausible, yet jointly inconsistent claims, which I call the *Lorry Driver Paradox*:

(1) The faultless driver is not morally responsible for the child's death.
(2) *Apology Principle*: one ought to apologise for something only if one is morally responsible for it.
(3) The driver ought to apologise for the child's death.

In this opening chapter, I shall motivate the *Lorry Driver Paradox* as a strong challenge to our thinking about moral responsibility and thereby present the central challenge for Part I of this book. I shall consider each of these individual claims in turn.

* Chapter one and chapter two are based on M Kiener, 'Strict Moral Answerability' (2024) 134(3) *Ethics* 360 (April). I thank the journal for the permission to reprint it as part of this book.

(1) THE FAULTLESS DRIVER IS NOT MORALLY RESPONSIBLE FOR THE CHILD'S DEATH

A wide range of approaches to moral responsibility would not consider the driver morally responsible. To begin with, the driver does not satisfy a *control condition* (*cf* Fischer and Ravizza 1998). The child appeared suddenly in front of his lorry and made averting the accident impossible, viz it was beyond human abilities and technical possibility not to hit the child. Moreover, the driver does not satisfy an *epistemic condition* (*cf* Robichaud and Wieland 2017). Let us suppose that he could not possibly have foreseen this accident. He drove in an industrial area where children had never played before. In addition, there was no prior point in time when the driver acted culpably and to which the accident could be *traced back* (*cf* Montminy 2019). The driver was completely sober and perfectly managed the maintenance of his vehicle. Finally, the accident does not reflect any *poor quality of will* (*cf* Strawson 1963). It does not show, to use Shoemaker's terminology, any defect in the driver's *character*, his *judgement*, or *regard* for others (Shoemaker 2015). As a result, the driver is not an appropriate target of those so-called reactive attitudes that many philosophers consider constitutive of moral responsibility. Thus, from across very different approaches to moral responsibility, we seem to have to conclude that, although the driver is causally involved in the accident, he is not morally responsible (Enoch 2012, 102; Cowley 2013, 130; Kim 2014, 206; Shoemaker 2015, 86; MacKenzie 2017, 96; F Santoni De Sio and Di Nucci 2018, 44–45; Kamtekar and Nichols 2019, 181).

(2) *APOLOGY PRINCIPLE*: ONE OUGHT TO APOLOGISE FOR SOMETHING ONLY IF ONE IS MORALLY RESPONSIBLE FOR IT

We say 'sorry' in a wide range of situations. Sometimes, we merely express *regret* about something without indicating our involvement in any way, and sometimes saying sorry is merely conforming to *etiquette*. Yet, in other situations, when we say 'sorry', we give a genuine apology.

Theorists have claimed that a genuine apology differs from regret and etiquette because it implies the admission of moral responsibility. For instance, Trudy Govier and Wilhelm Verwoerd claim that 'to apologize for an action is to admit that … one was responsible for it' (Govier and Verwoerd 2002, 69) and Daniel Shuman says that 'to be meaningful, an apology must … acknowledge responsibility' (Shuman 2000, 185; see also Gill 2000; S Harris, Grainger and Mullany 2006; N Smith 2008; Cunningham 2014). Theorists support this link between a genuine apology and moral responsibility in two main ways. First, an apology fails, and can be reasonably rejected, when the person apologising is either not morally responsible or fails to admit that responsibility; and if apologies can fail for that reason, they must imply responsibility. Secondly, when someone gives a genuine apology, this marks the end to a responsibility dispute: if we apologise, it may become inappropriate for other people to continue holding us answerable or blaming us (Owens 2012, 51–52; Bennett 2018). However, if apologies play this role, then – again – apologies must imply responsibility. Another way to support this argument would be to say that apologies can function like justifications and excuses: they can all bring a responsibility dispute to an end. But justifications and excuses[1] have this function only insofar as they presuppose moral responsibility. Thus, by parity of reasoning, we may assume that the same must be true for apologies and that they also presuppose moral responsibility.

Although theorists agree that apologies presuppose moral responsibility, stated in these general terms, they also rely on different conceptions of moral responsibility. Some theorists link apologies to the type of responsibility that implies blameworthiness, fault or guilt (Scanlon 2008; N Smith 2008, 150, ch 7). Support for linking apology to this conception of responsibility arises from the connection between apologies and forgiveness. When we apologise, it has been argued, we often seek forgiveness, or at least we give the person to whom we apologise a reason to forgive us (Hieronymi 2001; Gamlund 2010; Warmke 2016; Milam 2019; Difonzo, Alongi and Wiele 2020). But forgiving us only makes sense if we are also at fault or blameworthy in some way.

Yet, other theorists plausibly argue that an apology can also be owed when a person is not blameworthy or at fault in any way. As Matthew Kramer explained, an apology is owed when 'one's treatment of somebody else has fallen short of minimally acceptable standards' (Kramer 2005, 329), even if one is not blameworthy in the end (see also Sliwa 2019). Bennett points out that 'when one accidentally – though not negligently – treads on someone's toe one can owe the person an apology even though one is not blameworthy' (Bennett 2008, 115). And Antony Duff explains that 'what makes the apology necessary … is that I did what I in fact had good reason not to do' (Duff 2009a, 74), even if I am not blameworthy for acting as I did. In elaborating on their views, these theorists also state that apologies presuppose moral responsibility, but they operate with a conception of moral responsibility that does not imply blameworthiness. Rather, they focus on something like answerability or attributability (Watson 2004; Angela Smith 2005, 2015). This view finds support because, as mentioned previously, when one gives a genuine apology, this apology marks the end to a responsibility dispute, where such dispute could just amount to holding a person answerable rather than blaming the person or implying any fault. In addition, even in cases of responsibility without blameworthiness, apologies still play an important role, most notably as a means to renew or confirm one's commitment to shared

[1] I here understand excuses in contrast to exemptions or denials: excuses admit responsibility as answerability but reject blameworthiness, whereas exemptions or denials reject responsibility as answerability too (Duff 2009a).

moral values, to acknowledge the equal moral standing of those who have been harmed, to repudiate the harm one caused, or to pre-empt a disturbance in moral relations that could ensue from the harm if left without an apology (*cf* Bennett 2022; Sliwa 2019).

However, it is crucial to note that the two camps of theorists, ie those focusing on types of responsibility that imply blameworthiness and those separating responsibility from blameworthiness, need not contradict each other as far as a defence of the *Apology Principle* is concerned. They can converge on the view that moral responsibility (in one form or another) remains a necessary, yet not sufficient, condition of a fitting or obligatory apology.[2] Thus, we can rely on the arguments from theorists' different camps to support the more general claim in (2): one is *able* to give a genuine apology and one (*a fortiori*) also *ought* to give a genuine apology *only if* one is, or at least can be reasonably assumed to be, morally responsible. Thus, claim (2) seems correct as well.

(3) THE DRIVER OUGHT TO GIVE A GENUINE APOLOGY FOR THE CHILD'S DEATH

If the previous claims are true, viz that (1) the driver is not morally responsible and that (2) an apology presupposes moral responsibility, then it follows that (3), ie that the driver ought to apologise, is false. However, if we consider (3) *independently* and without relying on the previous sub-sections, we will find support for (3) too.

In the literature, people claimed that the driver who fails to apologise seems 'callous' (Cornford 2011, 45) and 'appalling' (Wolf 2001, 12), and they provided three main reasons why an apology is needed. First, there are *aretaic* reasons: given the involvement of the driver in the accident, it can become virtuous of the driver to apologise. In the case at hand, the driver is in a unique position to 'ease the pain or provide comfort to the grieving family' (Wolf 2001, 14), 'lessen the psychological burden [for them]' (MacKenzie 2017, 110), and help them to 'heal emotionally' (MacKenzie 2017, 113) with his apology. Thus, by apologising, the driver would act virtuously: the driver 'voluntarily benefits or tries to benefit others at cost to herself' (Wolf 2001, 14) and refuses to be a person who is 'more concerned with saving face than helping others' (MacKenzie 2017, 110).

Second, there are *deontic* reasons: it is not only virtuous to apologise, but also obligatory. Adam Smith, who described a case very close to that of the lorry driver long before Williams, said about such cases: 'To make no apology, to offer no atonement, is regarded as the highest brutality' (Adam Smith 2009, 125

[2] For the purposes of my argument, I remain neutral with regard to what exactly the sufficient conditions for an apology may be, and only state that responsibility is a necessary condition.

(Part II, Section III, Ch II)). Brutality implies that not apologising would be an offence to those who have been harmed as well as to their relatives. Tae Kim built on this aspect and argued that failing to apologise would 'gratuitously insult, offend, or humiliate others' (Kim 2014, 211), eg the child's family. Not apologising would fail to acknowledge the moral significance of the child's life.

Third, there are reasons linked to our status as a *person*. Wolf claimed that there is value in 'expressing our recognition that we are beings who are thoroughly in-the-world, in interaction with others whose movements and thoughts we cannot fully control, and whom we affect and are affected by accidentally as well as intentionally, involuntarily, unwittingly, inescapably, as well as voluntarily and deliberately' (Wolf 2001, 14). Wolf suggests that expressing this recognition and acknowledging our place as agents in the world requires not only accepting that harm stemmed from one's action, eg driving a lorry, but also apologising for that harm. Failing to do so clashes with a proper understanding of ourselves as persons who are in-the-world and also 'defines an approach to life that is unhealthy and undesirable' (Wolf 2001, 13).

Thus, when we bracket the question as to whether the driver is morally responsible for the moment, there are reasons to assume that the driver ought to give a genuine apology rather than merely express regret, viz there is support for claim (3). But to be clear: the support for each of the three propositions cannot be decisive. In fact, we have to reject or modify at least one of the propositions to avoid inconsistency. So, how should we do this?

2

*Strict Moral Answerability**

IN THIS CHAPTER, I want to develop a solution to the *Lorry Driver Paradox* based on the idea of *strict* moral answerability, which means, roughly, answerability without any requirement of fault. This approach is greatly indebted to Duff, who first introduced the idea of strict moral answerability (Duff 2009a). Unfortunately, however, Duff did not provide explicit support for his idea, which has led to strict moral answerability currently resting on contentious intuitions only, as Douglas Husak rightly notes (Husak 2010, 118). I wish to remedy this deficit and to provide the required support for the idea of strict moral answerability by showing how it can solve the *Lorry Driver Paradox*. But in so doing, I will also make substantial modifications to Duff's original proposal.

OUTLINE OF THE SOLUTION: STRICT MORAL ANSWERABILITY

Most theorists would accept claims (1) and (2) of the *Lorry Driver Paradox*, but reject claim (3), denying that the driver really ought to give a genuine apology, as opposed to merely expressing (agent-)regret (Scanlon 2008, 150; Bovens 2008). In this chapter, I will take the reverse strategy. I will accept claims (3) and (2) and suggest a modification of claim (1). More precisely, I offer the following solution that distinguishes between two notions of moral responsibility:

(1a) The faultless driver ***is not*** **morally liable, ie blameworthy**, for the child's death.
(1b) The faultless driver ***is*** **(strictly) morally answerable** for the child's death.
(2) *Apology Principle*: one ought to apologise for something only if one is morally **answerable** for it.
(3) The driver ought to apologise for the child's death.

From here, my main objective in the rest of this section is to explain and support claim (1b), ie the type of moral answerability I argue that the lorry driver has. In doing so, this chapter aims to resolve inconsistencies within the triad of claims, rather than construct a new logically valid argument to the conclusion that the driver ought to apologise. The claim that the driver ought to apologise is assumed as a given in this chapter, based on the arguments from chapter one. I will return

* Chapter one and chapter two are based on M Kiener, 'Strict Moral Answerability' (2024) 134 (3) *Ethics* 360 (April). I thank the journal for the permission to reprint it as part of this book.

to the reasons for apologising, as well as the relationship between answerability and apology, in subsequent chapters, particularly chapters three and four. I shall here also draw upon the version of the apology principle that frames responsibility in terms of answerability rather than culpability – a distinction also highlighted in chapter one.

THE DEFINITION AND THE CONDITION OF STRICT MORAL ANSWERABILITY

As a *definition* of moral answerability, I endorse the view that 'a morally responsible [ie answerable] agent is one who can intelligibly be asked to "answer for" her attitudes and conduct' (Angela Smith 2015, 103), where 'to answer for' means 'to give her (justificatory) reasons for thinking, feeling, or acting in the way she has' (Angela Smith 2015, 103) (Scanlon 2000, ch 6). So understood, morally answering for something requires, not a purely causal explanation of one's conduct (eg explaining the psychological causes behind one's action), but an explanation of one's motivation behind one's action and the good one saw in conducting oneself as one did. For this reason, the role of a morally answerable person is also different from the role of an eyewitness, who merely provides a detached report on what happened.

I also argue that moral answerability sometimes makes it not only intelligible, or fitting, to demand an answer from the responsible person, but also requires that the responsible person be under an *obligation* to provide such an answer, at least to those who have the standing to demand an answer.

In addition to this *definition* of moral answerability, I endorse the following *sufficient condition*: a person is morally answerable for harm if (i) the person caused the harm (causation-clause) and (ii) (s)he had a prospective obligation to guard against such harm (obligation-clause). I also presuppose that the person under consideration possesses the ability to be guided by the relevant reasons, which I interpret as the ability to recognise and respond to the reasons in favour of, as well as against, the conduct under consideration.[1] Yet, it is not required that the person was in any way at fault, ie by acting negligently, recklessly or even with intent.

My proposed *definition* of moral answerability is widely accepted and I will not claim any originality for it, whereas its *condition* will spark controversy and constitutes the novelty of my proposed view. It is also this condition that forms my proposed account into a view about *strict* moral answerability, where 'strict' means, roughly, that there is no requirement of fault on the part of the answerable person.

[1] Shoemaker emphasised the importance of the reasons against an action, which he called '"instead of" reasons'. I will discuss Shoemaker on this point later.

The lorry driver is an example of someone who is strictly morally answerable because he satisfies the sufficient condition of my proposal. He caused harm through his own driving (causation clause) and, *qua* driver, he had a prospective obligation to guard against that very harm, ie the harm of running over people with his vehicle (obligation clause). The driver also possessed the ability to be guided by the relevant reasons. The fact that he could not possibly have known about the whereabouts of the child, and that he was not in any way at fault, is immaterial to his strict moral answerability. Making responsibility *strict* in this fault-free way is, in fact, at the heart of my proposed solution to the *Lorry Driver Paradox*. Without it, the driver could not be considered morally answerable, and the inconsistency of the three propositions would persist.

To say that the driver is answerable means, following my definition, that it is not only intelligible and fitting to ask him to answer for the harm he caused, ie explain his motivating reasons behind acting as he did and reassure others that he took due care, but he may also be under a moral obligation to answer to the family of the victim. What is more, the driver's moral answerability may also involve a further cluster of what are often called secondary obligations connected to moral responsibility, such as the obligation to follow up on those whom he harmed or the obligation to apologise.

But to say that the driver is answerable does not imply that he is *liable* to moral blame or legal punishment. This is because people can be answerable for causing harm, yet still avert liability to blame, conviction, or punishment by providing an excuse or justification. Thus, I still adhere to the contrast between answerability and liability, which is also expressed in the distinction between claims (1a) and (1b) of my proposed solution to the paradox.

However, there is another, Hohfeldian sense of liability that can help further elucidate the concept of answerability (Hohfeld 1913).[2] According to Wesley Newcomb Hohfeld's well-known account, 'liability' is a person's susceptibility to have their legal relations changed by another person, which can include the imposition or removal of obligations. For instance, Peter has the liability to have an obligation imposed on him by Carol, if Carol is Peter's boss and can give Peter orders. Such liability, as any Hohfeldian liability, has a 'correlative' and an 'opposite'. The *correlative* of liability is power, ie the ability of one person to change legal relations for another person. In our example, Carol has the correlative power, ie the power to impose an obligation on Peter. The *opposite* of liability is immunity, ie the non-susceptibility to having legal changes being imposed on oneself by another. For instance, Peter has immunity against Tom, a co-worker who – unlike Carol – is not in a position to give Peter orders.

But Hohfeld's view can be extended beyond the law. In fact, it provides a useful resource to explain moral answerability too. In my view, an answerable person is (in the Hohfeldian sense) liable to requests for justification by certain

[2] Thanks to an anonymous reviewer for raising this point.

others. This means that, if such requests are made, the answerable person acquires a moral obligation to comply with them, respond, and explain his or her conduct. But prior to these requests, at least *sometimes*, this moral obligation (to explain, justify, etc) may not be there. An answerable person may not have to take the initiative, approach the victim or their family, and explain her conduct, especially if it is the case that they may not want that person to do so. The correlative of this liability is the power of certain others, who have the relevant standing, to demand an explanation or justification. The opposite of this liability would be the non-susceptibility to a demand for justification, which an answerable person forfeited through the causation of harm he had an obligation to guard against. So understood, Hohfeldian liability details the change in people's normative situation when they become morally answerable.

Applying this rationale to the lorry driver, we could say that the driver is not under an immediate obligation to explain, excuse or justify his conduct to the victim's family. Under certain circumstances, it is inappropriate if *he* forces his explanation onto the victim's family. But the driver is certainly liable to incur an obligation to explain, as soon as the victim's family requests an explanation. Thus, moral answerability includes forms of Hohfeldian liability, while still contrasting with liability to blame and punishment.

However, other aspects of moral answerability fall more clearly outside Hohfeld's proposed liabilities. For instance, the driver may have an obligation to *apologise*, independently of other people's requests for such an apology. Hence, Hohfeldian liabilities can elucidate only part of moral answerability.

In summary, then, my proposed view endorses a widely shared *definition* of moral answerability (which follows Angela Smith's formulation), a controversial *sufficient condition* (which makes answerability 'strict'), and an underappreciated *nuance* regarding a particular type of liability (which takes inspiration from Hohfeld). To explain the novelty of my proposed answerability view further, I will now draw three comparisons: one with traditional answerability views in moral philosophy, where I will mark stark contrasts; one with reverse burdens of proof in the criminal law, where I will highlight significant overlap; and one with the original proposal on strict moral answerability from Duff, where I will suggest two substantial modifications.

ANSWERABILITY IN CURRENT MORAL PHILOSOPHY

Differences in terminology aside, there is one point that answerability theorists in current moral philosophy accept, namely that being morally answerable for something requires that this something *reflect one's judgement*. Shoemaker says that '[o]ne is an answerable agent … in virtue of one's quality of judgment' (Shoemaker 2015, 82). Smith claims that '[i]n order for an agent to be answerable for something, … the thing in question must in some way reflect her own judgment or assessment of reasons' (Angela Smith 2015, 103). And Scanlon says that 'a person's judgment-sensitive attitudes are … those traits that are appropriate objects of moral criticism on my view (those that an agent is responsible for in the relevant sense)' (Scanlon 2000, 276).

For Shoemaker, a *harmful* action reflects an agent's evaluative judgement when, retrospectively, it is fitting for the agent to review his deliberative policies and take steps to ensure that similar things will not happen again (Shoemaker 2015, 67). For Smith and Scanlon, on the other hand, a harmful action reflects evaluative judgement when the action depends, for an ideally rational person, on an evaluative judgement in the sense that varying the judgement would also lead to variation in action, eg by precluding the harmful outcome (Angela Smith 2015, ch 6; Scanlon 2000, ch 6).

However, in neither of these views would the lorry driver be morally answerable for the accident. Regarding Shoemaker's view, the driver does not have a reason to change his deliberative policies, since – as the case stipulates – he behaved flawlessly. And Shoemaker indeed explicitly states that the agent-regret (in Williams's sense) that the driver feels is insufficient to establish answerability (Shoemaker 2015, 67–68). But in Smith's and Scanlon's views too, the driver is not morally answerable because the accident does not depend on (nor is it rationally sensitive to) the specific evaluative judgement that the driver had made at the time of his action. Even if we tweak the case so as to make the driver a moral saint, the accident – or so the case stipulates – would still have happened as it was merely the outcome of bad luck.

Thus, my own proposed answerability view differs from these views *extensionally*, as well as *intensionally*. My view differs extensionally because it gives a different verdict on Williams's case: unlike those other views, my view considers the lorry driver as morally answerable for the accident and the harm caused. My view differs intensionally because it gives an altogether different explanation of answerability. In my view, the condition of moral answerability is not the *reflection of judgement* but rather some form of *agential causation*, ie that the person caused a type of harm which he had an obligation to guard against. As a result, the primary objects of answerability in my view are not evaluative judgements, but actions and their consequences.

ANSWERABILITY IN THE CRIMINAL LAW

Let me now proceed to the second comparison, the one with criminal responsibility, and show how my view takes inspiration from the law. To recall, to solve the *Lorry Driver Paradox* in the way I indicated, I had to make moral answerability 'strict', and 'strict' is legal terminology.

In the law, both answerability, ie the obligation to explain one's conduct in court, as well as liability,[3] ie being appropriately subjected to conviction,

[3] I intend this in the ordinary, non-Hohfeldian sense.

punishment or an obligation to pay compensation, can be 'strict'. *Answerability* is strict when a person is obliged to answer in court solely by virtue of having performed a certain act, the *actus reus*, and independent from any, or some, specified *mens rea*, such as intent, negligence or recklessness. *Liability* is strict when – again, solely by virtue of having performed a certain act and independent of any, or some, *mens rea* – a person can be convicted, punished or obliged to pay compensation. Often scholars distinguish between *formal* and *substantive* strictness, where an offence is formally strict if it does not require proof of *some mens rea* element corresponding to an element in the actus reus, and it is substantively strict if does not require proof of *any mens rea* element. In this chapter, I am exclusively concerned with cases in which answerability, though not liability, is strict, and I will primarily focus on substantive strictness to exclude fault altogether (Duff 2009a, ch 10; Herring 2020, ch 4; Simester 2021, ch 13).

Cases of strict *answerability* arise in a very specific context in the criminal law, but I need to emphasise at the outset that these cases are the exception and not the rule. The rule is the presumption of innocence as stated, for instance, in article 6(2) of the Human Rights Act 1998: a person is innocent until proven guilty by the prosecution, which normally requires that the prosecution not only prove the *actus reus* but also the *mens rea*. This view was also notably expressed by Lord Sankey LC, who said that 'throughout the web of English criminal law one golden thread is always to be seen – that it is the duty of the prosecution to prove the prisoner's guilt' (*Woolmington v DPP* [1935] AC 462, 481). Section 1.12 of the Model Penal Code in the US echoes this view closely. Thus, until the prosecution discharges this burden of proof, a person has nothing to answer for in a criminal court of law.

Yet, the European Court of Human Rights and many domestic legal systems admit that the presumption of innocence, including the prosecution's burden of proof, is not absolute (*Salabiaku v France* [1988] 13 EHRR 379). There can be cases where the burden of proof shifts to the defendant in some regard, which means that there is 'a burden on the defendant to prove some matter, the effect of which is that he is not guilty of the offence charged' (Dennis 2005, 901). That matter is often the absence of a specific *mens rea*, eg that a person did not intend to defraud someone else, or that she did not act negligently or recklessly (see for instance, *Attorney-General's Reference (No 1 of 2004)* [2004] 2 CrAppR 424, from Dennis 2005, footnote 3). In such cases, a person can become criminally answerable after the prosecution has proved the *actus reus* only. The burden of disproving the required *mens rea* then rests with the defendant and is the only way to avoid conviction. In these cases, criminal *answerability* is strict (as it does not require the prosecution's proof of *mens rea*), while criminal *liability* is not (as it can be averted by the defendant's proof of due care, for instance).

Some examples might help to illustrate these points. Suppose a person engages in an activity from which she benefits, yet which also imposes special risks on others, eg because she runs a profitable yet risk-imposing factory. When the risks materialise and she causes harm to, say, her employees, then this fact alone could make her strictly answerable in a court of law, requiring her to prove that she took sufficient safety precautions, while it may still be insufficient to constitute any form of liability (see for instance, *Nimmo v Alexander Cowan & Sons* [1968] AC 107) (Duff 2009a, 243–246). Alternatively, suppose someone sells contaminated food. In this case she can be charged with the offence of '[s]elling food not of the nature or substance or quality demanded' under s 14 of the Food Safety Act 1990. But even then, she is not automatically criminally liable because s 21(1) also provides that it is 'a defence for the person charged to prove that he took all reasonable precautions and exercised all due diligence to avoid the commission of the offence'. Therefore, in such cases, *liability* still requires fault, or *mens rea*, and is therefore not 'strict'. But answerability arises irrespective of fault because it requires only the selling of contaminated food, and is therefore 'strict'.[4]

However, the law is also clear that making criminal answerability strict is only legitimate 'within reasonable limits', which means that the state must, first, pursue a *legitimate aim* and, secondly, do so in a *proportionate* manner (*Salabiaku v France* [1988] 13 EHRR 379, 388, para 28; Dennis 2005, 905; Herring 2020, 216–218). A legitimate aim would be facilitating efficient criminal justice in cases where, as Cory J in the Canadian Supreme Court[5] also pointed out, 'the enforcement of regulatory offences would be rendered virtually impossible if the Crown were required to prove negligence beyond a reasonable doubt' (*R v The Wholesale Travel Group Inc* [1991] 3 SCR 154, 246–247 (Cory J); Stumer 2010, 164–165). Additionally, pursuing a legitimate aim is *proportionate* only if, as Lord Bingham stressed (see Stumer 2010, 155), the 'rights of the individual [against wrongful conviction]' are sufficiently respected (see *McIntosh v Lord Advocate* [2003] 1 AC 1078 (PC); Stumer 2010, 155). For instance, reverse burdens of proof may be justified only when it is relatively easy for the defendant to discharge them, as it may be when, eg, it is only about showing that one had the required licence to engage in a certain regulated activity (Dennis 2005, 918–920), or when one would equip oneself with the means of answering in court just by discharging obligations to take due care, eg when a factory owner's required safety precautions already include record keeping (Duff 2009a, 244–246; Stumer 2010, ch 6).

However, the arguments for reverse burdens of proof and strict criminal answerability are not just pragmatic, ie relating to the efficiency of prosecuting and suppressing crime. There are also moral arguments as to why criminal answerability sometimes ought to be strict. Andrew Simester explained that

[4] See Duff (2009a).

[5] I deliberately quote from across different legal systems, ie European and Canadian, to carve out what is common ground concerning reverse burdens of proof.

'allocating the burden of proof is part of balancing the costs and risks of an activity between actors and potential victims' (Simester 2021, 302). For instance, if someone voluntarily engages in an optional activity from which she stands to gain but, in so doing, also imposes special risks on others, as when she runs a factory, it seems morally appropriate that she not only receives whatever benefits flow from this activity but also bears some of the costs and risks, including the burden of proof for the safety of his employees. Shifting the burdens of proof to a defendant and making criminal answerability strict in these cases is a matter of justly distributing benefits and burdens.

In addition, shifting burdens of proof is also, as Paul Roberts and Adrian Zuckerman argued, a matter of 'duties of citizenship [which] arguably imply that the accused should not be entirely absolved of all evidential labour' (Roberts and Zuckerman 2010, 244). Similarly, Duff says that an adequate view of allocating burdens of proof and strict answerability 'will involve an account of what it is reasonable for citizens to demand of each other, simply *qua* citizens, through the coercive apparatus of the criminal law' (Duff 2009a, 231). 'Reasonable' here is not a legal category but means what moral justification there is for certain demands in the criminal law. What these views state is that when we engage in certain risk-imposing activities, we owe it to others, ie those we harmed and our polity at large, that we not only take all the precautions against the existing risks but also answer in court and to them when things go wrong, quite independent of any proof of *mens rea* or other fault. *Mens rea* and fault will be relevant in assessing guilt and liability, but do not determine answerability.

This legal approach differs from the answerability views in current moral philosophy considerably. Unlike the latter, it sees answerability as strict, it does not require reflection of evaluative judgements, and it considers actions and not inner evaluative judgements as the primary object of answerability. Thus, unlike the latter, it does not understand answerability as a function of an agent's inner psychology but rather as a result of the impact she had as a real-world agent on others. The legal approach substitutes the intra-personal focus on evaluative judgements with an inter-personal focus on what citizens owe each other when engaging in certain activities.

Throughout all these contrasts, my proposed view on answerability resides with the legal approach rather than with moral philosophers' views. Yet, unlike the legal view, I propose a view of *moral* answerability rather than *criminal* answerability. I suggest that the strictness of answerability, understood as a legal concept, should be imported into our moral theory. Hence, my view suggests that the doctrines around strict criminal answerability are not just a peculiarity of the law but carve out a distinct type of moral answerability.

But there are also contrasts with the law which I need to highlight from the outset. In the criminal law, but not in morality, the prospects of conviction and punishment constrain the legitimate scope and nature of strict answerability. In addition, in the criminal law, but not in morality, the focus is restricted to a specific type of wrong, ie public wrongs. Moreover, in the criminal law, but not necessarily in morality, failing to discharge a burden of proof risks losing one's case and rendering one criminally liable. For these reasons, strict moral answerability may differ from strict criminal answerability in important respects. In morality, it remains an open question what the consequences are of an agent's inability to reassure others of her due diligence.

DIFFERENCES TO DUFF'S PROPOSAL

Finally, my approach is greatly indebted to Duff, who first introduced the idea that moral, and not just *legal* answerability, can be strict. Duff writes:

> For in moral contexts answerability is typically strict: I must answer morally for the harms that I cause even if I cause them through non-culpable accident or inadvertence. If I knock over your vase, or take your umbrella, you will rightly expect me to answer for what I have done. My answer might exculpate me, averting blame by showing that I lacked the moral equivalent of mens rea: I was pushed into the vase by a rushing child; I reasonably believed that it was my umbrella. But it is up to me to provide such an explanation – which is to say that I am morally answerable even for what I do through non-culpable accident or inadvertence. (Duff 2009b, 893–984; *cf* Duff 2009a, 220, 230)

Duff and I agree that moral answerability can be 'strict' in the sense that it does not require *mens rea* or fault. We therefore also both adopt an approach to moral answerability that, unlike the views from Smith, Shoemaker and Scanlon, does not require *reflection of judgement*. Yet, I disagree with Duff's view on strict moral answerability in two important respects, namely concerning (a) the role of uncertainty about a person's due diligence and (b) the scope of strict moral answerability.

Uncertainty

Duff explains cases of answerability as cases of accusations, eg 'accus[ations] of carelessness or negligence' (Duff 2009a, 71). Duff then elaborates that accusations against the lorry driver are apt and that the driver is morally answerable *when and because* his conduct raises a *question* about whether he exercised due diligence, ie when there is uncertainty about the moral quality of the conduct. But this understanding of strict moral answerability is problematic for three reasons.

First, on this view, it would follow that one person's answerability depends on other people's lack of knowledge. For if another person knew everything about the case, she could no longer 'accuse [the driver] of carelessness or negligence' (Duff 2009a, 71) or intelligibly raise the *question* about the driver's diligence. Yet, a person's moral responsibility does not depend on the ignorance of others in this way. I take this to be an implication of a very plausible principle about moral responsibility, which Alex Kaiserman called *Individualism*:

> Individualism: An agent A's degree of responsibility [or responsibility simpliciter] for some outcome *o* is *fully grounded* in facts about A, *o* and the relations between them. (Kaiserman 2021, 3598, emphasis added)

Accordingly, other people's knowledge alone cannot undermine one's otherwise existing moral responsibility.[6] Thus, making one person's answerability dependent on other people's uncertainty about what happened fails to capture an essential feature of moral responsibility.

Admittedly, in cases where one's sole purpose is to gather new information (eg when asking for directions to, say, a hotel), it may be inappropriate or pointless to ask questions to which one already knows the answers. But in the context of responsibility, things are different. Going back to the lorry driver case, even if the victim's family already knew exactly what happened and knew that the driver took due care, they still retain an entitlement, and possibly an emotional need, to hear that very fact *from the driver*, and the driver still owes them an answer in this regard. The family's knowledge does not undermine the driver's Hohfeldian liability to comply with their requests for justification and explanation, and their questions to the driver remain apt. Thus, we must not gloss over an important difference between asking questions in contexts of pure information gathering and holding people answerable in contexts of moral responsibility.

Second, Duff's view is ultimately unable to explain the answerability of the lorry driver. By introducing uncertainty about due diligence as a *condition* of moral answerability, Duff's view seems to imply that, since (*ex hypothesi*) there is no question about due diligence in this case, there is no answerability. There are simply no grounds left for 'accus[ations] of carelessness or negligence' and, for this reason, the driver could no longer be answerable. Thus, if we accept the link between uncertainty and answerability, we cannot account for the lorry driver's answerability in the first place.

Third, Duff's emphasis on uncertainty about the driver's diligence misrepresents answerability as being primarily an investigation into the driver's diligence. This is because it suggests that we are primarily in the business of investigating a factual question, ie finding out what actually happened and what the driver's role was in the chain of events under consideration. But if this is so, we would lack any principled reason to treat the answerable driver and a witness differently as they may both contribute to the investigation equally. Yet, we *do* treat them very differently, and for good reason. Morally answering for something is distinct from giving witness testimony. Moral answerability, unlike the role of

[6] Note that my argument only requires a weak version of Kaiserman's principle, which merely considers other people's *knowledge* (as opposed to further traits or facts about them) as irrelevant to one's own moral responsibility.

a witness, is not undermined if a person is unable to provide a good answer or assist an investigation. Moral answerability is about laying out one's motivating reasons for action and, in the case of the lorry driver, an acknowledgement of the moral significance of the harm caused, giving interpersonal assurance that one did not intend any harm, and potentially also giving an apology, by which one reaffirms the moral values underpinning the norms against harming others. Moral answerability requires taking a stance on the moral reasons and values that had a bearing on one's conduct and the moral relationship to others, but not necessarily any specific expertise on the chain of events under consideration. Duff's focus on the accident raising a question about negligence obscures these essential features about moral answerability and misleadingly portrays answerability too much like an investigation.

It is here that my view takes inspiration from Philip Pettit's political philosophy, in particular his idea of an 'assurance'. Pettit, in collaboration with John Braithwaite, describes an assurance as an expression by which one recognises the moral standing of others as equals and worthy of respect (*cf* Braithwaite and Pettit 1990, 60). In cases where one *interferes* with others, an assurance is also, more specifically, an acknowledgement that one's conduct ought to 'track the avowed interests of the individual interfered with' (Pettit 2005, 93), rather than 'interfere more or less as [one's] own will or judgment dictates' (Pettit 2005, 93). If one's interference causes *harm*, and it happens *non-culpably*, an assurance confirms one's continued commitment to shared values and mutual respect. In so doing, such an assurance helps victims overcome their emotional distress and dispel any residual fear of disrespect from the harm-causing person. It gives victims an additional and, in my view, interpersonally validated reason to 'look on that disadvantage [or harm] as a misfortune on a par with a natural accident; they do not have to see it as a token of domination … by other[s]' (Pettit 1997, 198). Therefore, an assurance can play an important role in maintaining our interpersonal moral relations, and it is such an assurance that, I argue, is also an essential part of moral answerability.[7] It shows what we expect from an answerable person even if they cannot provide any new information for others.

Explaining my view with reference to 'assurance' also highlights another clear contrast to Duff, because Duff used this term too, but in a different sense. Duff writes that 'we owe it to each other not merely to *ensure* that we act safely, but to *assure* each other that we are doing so, in a social world in which *we lack the personal knowledge* of others that could give us that assurance'

[7] Note that, although my view preserves the spirit of Pettit's idea as a particular form of mutual recognition, it also departs from Pettit's original proposal, most notably by transferring 'assurance' from a theory of freedom as non-domination to a theory about moral responsibility, by adopting a wider notion of interference that also includes accidental harm as in the lorry cases, and by concentrating primarily on moral rather than political or institutional matters.

(Duff 2009a, 170, final emphasis added). Here, Duff points again to a lack of knowledge of others when explaining why one might be answerable to them. Accordingly, giving an assurance as part of one's answer is then also about helping others to overcome their uncertainty about one's due diligence. So understood, an assurance is primarily a diligence protocol, or piece of evidence, and consequently Duff's two examples of an assurance in the case of driving are 'obtaining licences and obeying the speed limit' (Duff 2009a, 246). By contrast, I emphasise that an assurance requires not evidence but an expression of moral commitment, namely a renewed or confirmed commitment to shared moral values and mutual respect; and I hold that mere diligence protocols would be a truncated and, in the context of answerability, morally inappropriate form of assurance.

In summary, then, my proposal differs from Duff's view as I do not require there to be uncertainty about a person's diligence. Even in cases with perfect information about the lorry driver's due diligence, the driver can still be answerable for his non-negligent causation of harm. What is required in my view is only that he caused harm and had an obligation to guard against such harm.

Scope of Answerability

The second difference between Duff's view on strict moral answerability and my proposal is that Duff's view implies a commitment to JJ Thomson's *Harm Thesis*, which I reject.[8] To see this, and how it leads to a different scope of answerability, consider a central example in Duff's account.

Duff imagines a case in which he flicks a light switch and, through some freakish and unpredictable chain of events, causes an explosion that kills someone. He claims that, in this case, he would be strictly morally answerable for the death and says: 'I surely owe it to others, most obviously the victim's family, to explain how I came to cause his death; and, whilst my explanation averts liability, it admits responsibility [as answerability], in that it admits that I must answer for causing his death' (Duff 2009a, 75). Unfortunately, Duff only appeals to intuitions to support this conclusion, but I think we can reconstruct a more explicit argument for his view.

The central principle in Duff's account is that 'retrospective responsibility depends on prospective responsibility' (Duff 2009a, 65). Duff repeatedly stresses

[8] I shall concentrate on Duff's published work here and regard such work as representing his considered view. Yet, during the online workshop 'Responsibility and Control' in 2021, which I organised during my position on the ERC project Roots of Responsibility, Duff suggested potentially revising his position in a way that my conclusion aligns with. If Duff modified his view accordingly, this section could turn from a critique into additional support for, or specification of, Duff's new view.

that 'I am responsible for (and only for) those [risks and actions] … in relation to which I had a suitable prospective responsibility' (Duff 2009a, 70), ie a prospective obligation not to cause the harm in question (Duff 2009a, 30, 70, 75). However, this principle alone does not yet lead to Duff's intended conclusion in the explosion case. So, what else is needed?

I argue that Duff implicitly relies on a central view from Thomson's discussion of rights, namely what Thomson calls the 'Harm Thesis: We have claims against others that they not cause us harm' (Thomson 1990, 228). The *Harm Thesis* focuses on 'claims', ie claim-rights. But since claim-rights correspond to obligations, we can also reformulate the *Harm Thesis* as saying that we have (prospective) obligations owed to others that we not cause them harm. The distinctive features of Thomson's *Harm Thesis* are, first, that claim-rights and obligations are *objective* in the sense that they do not depend on what agents know, believe or have evidence for; and second, that Thomson does not further qualify types of harm and states a general right not to harm others, full stop. To illustrate this view, Thomson presents a case called *Day's End*, in which a person, B, flicks a switch and, through a freakish causal chain, causes severe harm to another person, A, just as in Duff's example.

Thus, Thomson's view is exactly what Duff needs in order to say that, in his imagined case of the freakish explosion, he infringes a prospective obligation by causing the explosion. Once Thomson's view is made explicit, we arrive at the following argument:

1. **Duff's Principle:** I am retrospectively responsible for some harm if and only if I had a prospective obligation not to cause such harm.
2. **Thomson's Harm Thesis** (Obligation-Version): I have a prospective obligation not to cause harm to others, full stop, including the obligation not to kill others through freakish explosions.
3. **Duff's Conclusion**: If I kill others through a freakish explosion, I am strictly morally answerable for their deaths.

Unfortunately, Duff's commitment to Thomson's *Harm Thesis* is problematic, given the criticisms that have been raised against Thomson's view. Two of them strike me as particularly strong.

To begin with, we simply do not have an obligation not to cause harm, full stop. For instance, consider a situation in which someone opens a new business and drives their competitor out of the market. Doing so could cause great harm to their competitor. Yet, driving a competitor out of business by building one's own business does not violate (or even infringe) the competitor's rights. Or suppose someone registers early to receive an organ donation. She may thereby fairly (let us assume) deprive someone else of the opportunity to receive an organ. Even if the latter person dies, that person's right is not necessarily violated (or even infringed) (Quong 2015). Examples like these seem to show that, in a situation of fair competition for scarce resources (eg custom, organs, jobs, etc), there is no unqualified right not to be harmed and no unqualified corresponding obligation not to harm.[9]

Furthermore, as Jonathan Quong highlighted, claim-rights and their corresponding obligations are distinctively *second-personal* in the sense that they are constrained by what people can reasonably demand from each other (Quong 2015, 258). However, Thomson's view, Quong adds, neglects this second-personal dimension because it enables people to demand from each other what no one can possibly achieve. It is impossible to comply with the *Harm Thesis* and to avoid *any* harm to others. What is more, it is also unreasonable to expect people even to *guard or take precautions* against any kind of risk of harm, however unforeseeable it is. But if so, Quong argues and I agree, then Thomson's conception of claim-rights and obligations reduces them to some form of objective constraints on action and fails to capture their distinctive second-personal dimension.

Based on these two criticisms, I reject Thomson's *Harm Thesis* and, as a result, also the reconstructed argument behind Duff's view that was founded on it. Instead, I offer a more restricted view. I claim that people are morally answerable for harm if and only if it was a *type of harm* that they had a *specific obligation to guard against*. There are two changes in comparison to Duff's proposal.

First, I argue only that we have obligations regarding *specific types* of harm, and thereby avoid the first criticism against Thomson's *Harm Thesis* that Duff inherited. In Williams's initial case, the lorry driver caused a type of harm which he, *qua* driver, had a special obligation to guard against. When driving lorries, or any other vehicle, people are obliged to make sure they do not hit or kill people. The risk of such a harm is essential to driving and known by the driver in advance. But the explosion in Duff's example is very different and I assume that, when flicking a light switch, we do not have a prospective obligation to guard against the risks of explosions.

Second, the obligation-clause in my view states that a person had an obligation to *guard against* a certain type of harm, rather than (as Duff suggests) an

[9] In response, Thomson could point to her view that the right not to be harmed can be waived or forfeited (Thomson 1990, 234) and, thus, it is not as unrestricted as it seems. When consenting to participation in a boxing match, a person can waive their right not to be harmed in ways inherent in this activity. Moreover, when unjustly attacking someone else, a person can forfeit their right not to be harmed as part of proportionate self-defence. In all these cases, harming a person would not violate (or even infringe) a right. However, forfeiture and waivers are not enough to account for the aforementioned counterexamples. *Forfeiting* a right requires wrongdoing or posing an illegitimate threat, which is absent in the examples concerning businesses, organ allocation and romantic break-ups. *Waiving* a right, on the other hand, normally requires an explicit act, which is also absent in the aforementioned examples. But even if we can waive rights implicitly, it is *ad hoc* to claim that every time we feel there is no right not to be harmed then the said right is implicitly waived. Hence, the counterexamples show that there is no general right not to be harmed. Any adequate theory of rights needs to provide an explanation of these cases and Thomson's view seems unable to do so.

obligation *not to cause it*, full stop. This change protects my view against the second objection to Thomson's *Harm Thesis* because guarding against certain risks is certainly what people can reasonably demand from each other. Thus, in my view, obligations can retain their distinctive second-personal characteristic that Quong highlighted.

Hence, unlike Duff, I offer a view of strict moral answerability that is independent from Thomson's *Harm Thesis* and its potential shortcomings. My view thereby confirms the lorry driver's strict moral answerability without also implying strict moral answerability in the explosion case. As a result, my view can distinguish, at least more clearly than Duff's view can, between genuine moral responsibility (lorry driver) and mere causal responsibility (explosion case).[10] Moreover, my view does not imply, as Duff's view seems to, that strict moral answerability and fitting agent-regret are co-extensive. In Duff's view, we seem to be answerable whenever we cause harm and therefore have reason to feel agent-regret, whereas my more restricted approach to obligations still allows us to identify cases like the explosion example, in which there is fitting agent-regret but no moral responsibility.

OBJECTION: STRICT ANSWERABILITY IS A CONTRADICTION IN TERMS

So far, I have explained the *Lorry Driver Paradox* as a novel challenge to how we think about moral responsibility and I have elaborated on how the idea of strict moral answerability can solve this paradox, including an explanation of the novelty of my specific proposal. Before I conclude, I will first address an important and fundamental objection from Shoemaker against the idea that moral answerability can be strict.

In response to Duff's account, Shoemaker argued that strict answerability is a contradiction in terms: either one is answerable, but then there is no strictness, or there is strictness but no answerability. To support this view, Shoemaker asks us to imagine the case where I (as the protagonist of the example) open a door and thereby knock over your vase that was standing behind it. Although my action caused harm, it was completely inadvertent and without fault. Just like the lorry driver, I did not and could not have known what harm my action would bring. Shoemaker claims, *pace* Duff, that I am not morally answerable in this case and explains this as follows:

> [I]n moral answerability there is an implicit completion of the accusatory question 'Why did you Φ?' which is rarely made explicit but is nevertheless crucial: 'Why did

[10] Let me clarify, however, that on my view too, it would still be inadequate to consider the light switch case as a mere insurance matter. It is fitting and morally expected that the person under consideration express agent-regret. Yet, this still falls short of moral answerability. The person is not under an obligation to apologise.

> you Φ in light of the reason(s) not to Φ?' My having a genuine answer to this question depends on my having access to those reasons for not Φ-ing. If I did not know you had placed the vase outside the door I was about to go through, I lacked access to that reason for not opening the door, so despite the fact that I did have a reason for voluntarily opening the door, I had no reason to refrain from doing so. (Shoemaker 2013, 164)

Thus, in Shoemaker's view, being answerable for Φ-ing requires access to the reasons *against* Φ-ing, not only to the reasons in favour of Φ-ing. Shoemaker does not explain what exactly he means by 'access', but he seems to imply both the *ability* and *opportunity* to respond to those 'against'-reasons or, as he calls them elsewhere, 'instead-of'-reasons (Shoemaker 2015). In the vase example, I may have had the ability to respond to the relevant reasons since I possessed the required mental capacities to be responsive to the relevant reasons. Yet, I lacked the opportunity to do so since I could not have known about the location of your vase. Therefore, Shoemaker claims, I am not morally answerable for knocking over your vase. But if this is true, Shoemaker concludes, 'there could be no strict answerability ..., for the strictness [implying a lack of opportunity] is precisely what would render the accused agent *not* answerable' (Shoemaker 2013, 165). Thus, I am not morally answerable for breaking your vase and, according to the same arguments, the lorry driver is not morally answerable for killing the child.

Shoemaker is certainly right to require *ability*. The lack of certain mental capacities needed to be responsive to the reasons against Φ-ing does indeed undermine being answerable for Φ-ing. In later work, Shoemaker gives a convincing example for this view. He discusses the case of a humanoid who is only responsive to reasons in favour of Φ-ing and completely insensitive to the existing reasons against Φ-ing. Shoemaker plausibly claims that the lack of this ability to respond to reasons against Φ-ing undermines answerability. Here is what he says (and I ask the reader to read 'incapable' as 'unable' or 'lacking the ability (rather than opportunity)'):

> if one is *genuinely incapable* of seeing the reasons in favor of anything other than Φ, one is obviously incapable of including them in one's deliberations or judging as to their relative worth, and so, it would seem, one could not give a sufficiently robust answer to the answerability demand about one's doing Φ, even if one took oneself to have justifying reasons in favor of Φ. (Shoemaker 2015, 76, emphasis added)

However, Shoemaker's requirement that there also needs to be an *opportunity* becomes the point of contention. Duff responded to Shoemaker's objection, first, by accepting the starting point, namely that a person is answerable for some harm if and only if she had 'access' to the reason not to do it. But Duff then offered a different take on what 'access' means. He says: 'what matters is that ... that reason [not to do it] is accessible to me, in the sense that I can understand it with hindsight, and could have understood it at the time' (Duff 2019, 171). I take this interpretation of access as pointing us to an *ability* to understand the relevant reasons at the time of the action, rather than an *opportunity* to have a fair chance to appreciate the reasons in the situation. In other words, Duff accepts the requirement of an ability, but completely rejects the requirement of an opportunity.

I think Duff's reply remains unsatisfactory because it simply restates his position without addressing Shoemaker's important concern. I will therefore suggest a different reply.[11]

The vase example is an especially difficult case because it is unclear what our prospective obligations are in such a situation. Are we really obliged to take special precautions for the protection of vases and similar objects when opening doors, other things being equal? Duff seems to think so and therefore argues that there is strict moral answerability in the vase case. I do not have any firm intuitions, but I tend towards a view which I also take to be Shoemaker's view, namely that such an obligation to protect vases does not exist. And if no such obligation exists, then there is also no moral answerability for breaking the vase.[12]

Yet, and this is the important and overlooked point in the dispute between Duff and Shoemaker: the conclusion that I am not answerable for knocking over the vase is compatible with the view that the lorry driver is answerable for hitting the child. The relevant difference is that, in the vase case, there was no obligation to guard against breaking vases, whereas in the lorry driver case there was indeed an obligation to guard against hitting people.

So, assessing the cases at hand requires that we do not conflate two different questions, namely: (i) what our prospective obligations in the vase example are, and (ii) whether moral answerability can *ever* be strict. Shoemaker may be right to deny a relevant prospective obligation in the vase case and, consequently, also right to deny answerability. But this does not license the rejection of strict moral answerability altogether. Shoemaker's example of the vase is within a grey area, between the clear (in my view) moral answerability of the lorry driver and the clear (in my view) absence of moral answerability in the explosion case. Shoemaker mispresents his claims as an objection to strict moral answerability as such when they are actually only an invitation to clarify our prospective obligations.

Two aspects of my reply to Shoemaker are worth emphasising. First, this reply is not available to Duff's proposal since Duff's commitment to Thomson's

[11] This reply will remain close to core ideas in Duff's overall account, most notably to the principle that retrospective responsibility depends on prospective responsibility and the view (which I assume Duff would share) that there can be unclarity about what our prospective responsibilities, ie our prospective obligations, are.

[12] Note, however, that my proposed view is not committed to any specific view about what our obligations are. I only make the more general claim that what one is answerable for depends on what one's prospective obligations are. This view is compatible with different first-order normative theories of obligations, and I take it to be a strength of my account of responsibility that it does not prejudice what obligations we have.

Harm Thesis forces him to assume that the person knocking over the vase is morally answerable. By contrast, my view can deny answerability in the vase case without giving up strict answerability in the lorry driver case, and may therefore have another advantage over Duff's proposal. Second, unlike Duff's reply, my response to Shoemaker can still accept that there is *some* requirement of an *opportunity*, and not just ability, to respond to reasons. Here is why.

Whenever we have a prospective obligation to guard against a certain type of harm, eg not to hit people with our cars, we ought to, and also can, take meaningful precautions, such as ensuring the maintenance of our vehicles, driving within the speed limit, and so on. The important implication here is that taking these precautions is one way to respond to the reasons not to hit people because these precautions are ultimately motivated, justified and demanded by these reasons. Therefore, whenever we have a prospective obligation, and thus an *opportunity* to take meaningful precautions, we also have an *opportunity* to respond to the reasons not to hit people. Hence, it is mistaken to think that we only have an opportunity to respond to the reasons against causing harm shortly before or during an action, and only when we can anticipate, on this specific occasion, that our conduct will cause harm.

Hence, I claim that there are two interpretations of 'opportunity'. Shoemaker suggests that an 'opportunity' requires a fair chance to respond to the reasons against some form of conduct *in* the situation at hand, while I suggest that an 'opportunity' in the relevant sense also arises when there is a fair chance to take meaningful precautions. Thus, I diverge from Shoemaker's original view by adding another interpretation of 'opportunity'. But I still accept, as Shoemaker does, (a) that answerability requires 'access' to reasons, (b) that the relevant reasons are those in favour as well as against some conduct, and (c) that 'access' to those reasons requires the ability as well as the opportunity to respond to reasons. So understood, my reply to Shoemaker could even be understood as a further development of Shoemaker's view. My view allows Shoemaker to uphold its negative part, namely the criticism of Duff's conception of strict moral answerability, which Shoemaker initially addressed, while also adding a positive angle by showing how a second reading of 'opportunity' can be used to support another – ie my – form of strict moral answerability. It may be that Shoemaker ultimately rejects the notion of opportunity that I proposed. But if so, we will disagree on this specific point rather than the general principle regarding 'access' to reasons. In any case, or so I argue, strict answerability (in the version I propose) is not a contradiction in terms.

CONCLUSION

This chapter developed a novel view of strict moral answerability as a solution to the novel challenge of the *Lorry Driver Paradox*. In so doing, I aimed to provide explicit support for the idea of strict moral answerability, which we previously lacked. I also showed how my proposal on strict moral answerability differs from current views on moral answerability in the philosophical literature, that it shares certain key features of strict criminal answerability in the context of reverse burdens of proof, and how it improves upon Duff's original proposal. Finally, I addressed a key objection from Shoemaker and argued that my view on strict moral answerability is consistent with the view that answerability requires both the ability and some opportunity to respond to relevant reasons. On this basis, I conclude that we need to acknowledge strict moral answerability as a form of genuine moral responsibility. But this conclusion may face other challenges if alternative solutions to the *Lorry Driver Paradox* become available.

3

Taking Responsibility as a Normative Power

IN THIS CHAPTER, I shall test an alternative solution to the *Lorry Driver Paradox*, based on the idea of taking responsibility as a normative power, that is, roughly, the idea of making oneself responsible by mere declaration. To do so, I start from David Enoch's ingenious presentation of this idea but then connect it to the *Lorry Driver Paradox* in a way that generates novel and distinctive support. Finally, I raise two objections against Enoch's model of taking responsibility and argue that responding to them requires two substantial modifications, which then lead me to my own and novel proposal on this normative power of taking responsibility. Moreover, as before, I shall highlight another crucial parallel to legal responsibility.

OUTLINE OF THE SOLUTION: TAKING RESPONSIBILITY

Enoch provides an elaborate discussion of the normative power of taking responsibility. Enoch does not focus solely on the lorry driver case but rather considers a variety of cases, and he does not address anything like the *Lorry Driver Paradox*. However, despite these differences between his approach and mine, Enoch's discussion of William's case suggests an innovative solution and I shall use his thoughts as the starting point of my discussion.

Enoch explicitly accepts claim (1) of the *Lorry Driver Paradox*: the driver, he says, is 'not [morally] responsible' (Enoch 2012, 102). Moreover, for the purposes of my argument, I shall assume that Enoch also accepts (2), ie that one ought to apologise only if one is morally responsible. (Although Enoch does not explicitly address such a claim, it would at least be consistent with his overall view.[1]) Yet, even if we assume that Enoch accepts (1) and (2), Enoch could then also still accept (3), ie that the lorry driver ought to apologise. This is because Enoch claims that, although the driver is not automatically morally responsible, he is 'morally required to *take* responsibility, where this taking makes a difference to the responsibility-facts' (Enoch 2012, 100). Taking responsibility,

[1] He comes closest in Enoch (2012, 118).

as Enoch understands it, is a normative power, like consenting or promising. Enoch elaborates:

> There is room in logical space for a normative power to make oneself – by an act of will – responsible for something like … the unintended and unforeseen consequences of one's actions [ie the lorry driver case] where one would not have been responsible for that thing but for the act of taking responsibility. (Enoch 2012, 95)

But if Enoch is right about this, morality requires that the driver not only take responsibility but also, as a consequence, apologise once responsible. Thus, if the driver follows through with what morality requires of him, it follows that (3) the driver ought to apologise for the child's death.

Thus, Enoch's ideas about taking responsibility can help us to the following solution to the *Lorry Driver Paradox*. Immediately after the accident, at time T1, the driver is not morally responsible. Yet, he is under a duty to *take* responsibility, ie to make himself responsible. Thus, after doing so, at time T2, he becomes responsible and, because of that 'difference to the responsibility-facts' (Enoch 2012, 100), he now ought to apologise. Accordingly, a possible solution could come down to the following (with changes in bold font).

(1) **Initially,** the faultless driver is not morally responsible for the child's death.
(2) *Apology Principle:* one ought to give a genuine apology for something only if one is morally responsible for it.
(3) The driver ought to **take responsibility and, having done so, subsequently also** give a genuine apology for the child's death.

Although Enoch considers taking responsibility and apologising to be conceptually distinct acts, and I shall follow him in my analysis in this respect, he also suggests that apologising can be part of the ontology of taking responsibility, meaning that one can take responsibility *by* apologising (Enoch 2012, 98). Moreover, he seems to suggest that at least in some situations, apologising may be the most appropriate way to take responsibility. If this is the case for the lorry driver, then his assertion that the driver has reason, or is even 'morally required', to take responsibility may also imply that the driver has reason to apologise. Understood in this way, the solution to the *Lorry Driver Paradox* may not only resolve the inconsistency within the triad of claims but also provide a further argument as to why the driver ought to apologise.

Furthermore, when Enoch talks about taking responsibility, he has a particular conception of responsibility in mind. Thus, unlike in my earlier exposition of the *Lorry Driver Paradox* in chapter one, where I remained neutral towards various conceptions of moral responsibility, Enoch's solution requires us to take sides. For Enoch does not think of moral responsibility in terms of blameworthiness (Enoch 2012, 115–116); rather, he thinks of responsibility in terms of owing an explanation, justification, or apology. He says:

> A is responsible (in this sense) for X to P if and only if, X is wrong or otherwise morally problematic, A owes it to P to justify X (or the relevant X-related thing), or

> to offer an excuse for it, or to apologize for it, or to explain it, or something of this sort. (Enoch 2012, 118)

Thus, in Enoch's view moral responsibility also consists in a type of moral *answerability*, ie being the appropriate addressee for requests for a justification or excuse for some action. He does not explain the idea of such answerability in detail but assumes that harming others may entail an obligation to apologise. Moreover, Enoch suggests that this type of answerability is widely accepted as a form of moral responsibility. For now, I accept this specification, but I shall later come back to it and suggest that it needs modification.

In addition, Enoch stresses that the moral responsibility he focuses on still pertains to *retrospective* responsibility, ie responsibility for things that happened in the past, rather than *prospective* responsibility, ie responsibility for things that will happen in the future. But, despite his claim that the *object* of such responsibility (ie the accident) is retrospective and lies in the past, Enoch still stresses that *the effects* of taking such responsibility, ie becoming morally answerable, are prospective, ie they lie in the future: *only from the moment of taking responsibility* does one become answerable for what happened. Before the act of taking responsibility, one was not obliged to answer to others. This emphasis on the retrospective nature of responsibility is important and makes Enoch's proposal distinctive.

Furthermore, and this is key for Enoch's take on Williams's case, the lorry driver not only has the *power* to take responsibility but also the *duty* to do so. Enoch says that the driver is 'morally required to take responsibility' (Enoch 2012, 100) and if he fails to discharge this duty, he will act wrongly. Enoch himself does not explain why the lorry driver has such a duty, but others who support his view have added that taking responsibility may be obligatory because there is some kind of 'duty of decency or negative duty not to insult, offend, or humiliate' (Kim 2014, 211), and they have argued that only by taking responsibility and apologising can the driver avoid insulting his victim and the victim's family. (This emphasis on duty is another point to which I shall return later.)

However, Enoch stresses that one cannot take responsibility for absolutely anything. For instance, one cannot take responsibility for the movements of the planets. Only if something is in the 'penumbra of our agency' (Enoch 2012, 95, 100–102), as Enoch puts it, is it possible to take responsibility for it. This penumbra is the grey area between the things we are clearly responsible for (eg fully controlled, intentional acts) and the things we are clearly not responsible for (eg the movements of the planets).

Unfortunately, in the end Enoch also leaves the notion of such a penumbra vague. For the purposes of this chapter, I want to be more specific on when something falls into this penumbra so that people become able to take responsibility for it. I suggest two conditions.

First, and to exclude cases one would be answerable for anyway, I suggest that Shoemaker's influential test of answerability must fail. Shoemaker claims that, in cases of harmful or wrongful conduct, answerability attracts the kind of regret that comes with 'a motivational impulse to change one's deliberative policies in the future' (Shoemaker 2015, 67). Shoemaker calls this 'agential regret' and explicitly contrasts it with Williams's 'agent-regret', which need not include any motivation to change one's deliberative policies at all (Shoemaker 2015, 68). Thus, this test requires that a person has good reason to change their deliberative policies. In the case of the lorry driver, as Shoemaker also says, this test is not met as the driver does not have reason to change his deliberative policies.

Second, and to exclude what we could not possibly be responsible for, like the movements of the planets, I suggest that a *denial* must be unavailable. A denial is a defence asserting that the agent did not perform the act or omission, hold the belief, or engage in the behaviour in question. In my interpretation, a denial also implies that the agent had no special connection to the entity, agent or event that caused the outcome (eg through causal contributions, complicity, incentivisation, or a special social relationship like parenthood). Thus, so understood, a denial is a broad refusal of any agential involvement. As such, a denial is different from other defences. For instance, the defence of an exemption relies, not on the rejection of agential involvement, but on a lack of control or the absence of standing for others to hold the agent responsible. The defences of justifications and excuses, meanwhile, acknowledge answerability but aim to mitigate or avoid liability to blame or legal redress. Thus, a denial distinctly stands out by wholly denying any agential involvement. Therefore, even without a denial, the agent may still claim other defences.

I propose that we understand Shoemaker's concept of answerability (as detected by his test) and the defence of a denial as contraries rather than contradictories. This means they can both be absent, but they cannot both be present. Conceiving them as contraries rather than contradictories opens up the space for things we can take responsibility for.

By way of further elaboration: two propositions, P and Q, are *contradictories* when they cannot be simultaneously true or simultaneously false; one must be true and the other false. In contrast, propositions P and Q are *contraries* when they cannot be simultaneously true but can be simultaneously false. Shoemaker's answerability and the defence of a denial are not contradictories because the propositions affirming their respective presence or applicability cannot both be true at the same time. However, they can both be false, and hence are contraries. In other words, an agent may not satisfy Shoemaker's answerability test, yet still also not have a denial. Such cases include, for instance, harmful outcomes which are either the consequence of a materialised risk that is normally associated with certain activities, such as the risk of hitting people while driving, as in the lorry driver case, or the consequence of some other intentional activity, which can include cases like Thomson's *Day's End*, in which someone intentionally flicks a light switch, which then (completely unforeseeably and freakishly) causes someone else to suffer a burn (Thomson 1990). These two examples are not meant to provide an exhaustive list, and they also leave other important questions open, including questions about the required level of causal proximity or causal contribution, which I cannot discuss in detail here. Yet, I hope they highlight two distinctive kinds of cases in which there is an agential connection between a person's conduct and a harmful outcome, while Shoemaker's test for answerability can still fail.

Accordingly, I argue, when both conditions are met (ie no Shoemaker answerability and no denial), a certain harmful outcome falls into the penumbra of someone's agency so that this person becomes able to take responsibility for it.[2] Note that my focus here is on the conditions under which people *can* take responsibility, rather than providing a comprehensive account of the conditions under which they *ought* to take responsibility. A full exploration of the latter, which would constitute an ethics of taking responsibility, is a topic for further research. However, I shall identify reasons for taking responsibility, and hence the 'ought' to take responsibility, later in this chapter, namely when comparing legal and philosophical scholarship on taking responsibility.

But before I proceed, let me clarify the differences between my approach and Enoch's original view at the outset. Enoch's dialectic is very different from mine. Enoch supported the idea of a normative power of taking responsibility by discussing a range of very different cases, including cases where people take responsibility for their country, or where a parent takes responsibility for a misdeed of their teenage son (ie taking responsibility for the actions of *others*). And he claims that his proposal in relation to the normative power of taking responsibility can 'vindicate common intuitions' and 'capture rather nicely the phenomenology' of all these rather different cases, and thus align with an 'intuitive date' (Enoch 2012, 95, 103, 111). Enoch's discussion of examples is insightful and imaginative. Yet, his intuitive verdicts have been challenged in various ways and leave the idea of taking responsibility dependent on contestable intuitions. By contrast, I have tried to isolate the idea of taking responsibility in just one case, or type of case, namely that of Williams's lorry driver (ie taking responsibility for one's own actions or their consequences). And instead of appealing to moral phenomenology, I have aimed to contribute a distinct argument for recognising a normative power of taking responsibility by showing that it can help us solve a puzzle, namely the inconsistent triad in the *Lorry Driver Paradox*. So, as well as elaborating Enoch's view to some extent, I have placed the idea of taking responsibility in a different dialectic (or argumentative context), hoping that this could further increase its support. Doing so was meant to provide friendly yet distinctive contributions to Enoch's initial idea.

To explain the novelty of the idea of a normative power of taking responsibility further, I will now draw two comparisons: one with accounts in moral

[2] I here only focus on causing harm rather than omitting to prevent harm. While, I remain open to the possibility that one can take responsibility for harm that one omitted to prevent, this question lies beyond the scope of this chapter.

philosophy, where I will mark significant differences, and one with the legal doctrine of state immunity in public international law, where I will find crucial inspiration.

TAKING RESPONSIBILITY IN MORAL PHILOSOPHY

The phrase 'taking responsibility' has been used in philosophy in various senses, eg in the sense of accepting a pre-existing responsibility (as our everyday use of the phrase often suggests), as a process of psychological integration (Frankfurt 1975), as a process of moral development (Fischer and Ravizza 1998), as an explanation as to why 'one person might properly blame herself more than another whose action was equally faulty' (Wolf 2001, 17), as some 'disposition … [embedded in] the genuine and legitimate needs of our relationships' (Mason 2018, 178), or as a distinctively first-personal emotional response to one's own actions (Bero 2020). But none of these views describes 'taking responsibility' as a genuine normative power by which people can (in retrospect) make themselves responsible merely by declaring that they are. Thus, the proposal under consideration remains significantly different from the philosophical mainstream.

However, the current proposal is not just *different* from previous accounts, it also seems to *contradict* a major paradigm in the philosophy of responsibility. This paradigm is the view that responsibility is fully grounded in the facts about how an action or outcome was brought about, but cannot be affected, changed or even constructed at a later point. Mason succinctly summarises this view: 'Responsibility cannot be taken after the fact, because responsibility is determined by the history of the act, and that is essential to the concept of responsibility' (Mason, 2023, 364). We may call this view *Historicism*, as it holds that responsibility is fully grounded in the facts about how an action or outcome was brought about, but cannot be affected, changed or created at a later point.

Despite controversy and disagreement in the well-trodden debate on moral responsibility, it seems that this view has not been a point of contention. Consider so called control theorists of responsibility. In their book 'Responsibility and Control: A Theory of Moral Responsibility', John Fischer and Mark Ravizza argue that to be morally responsible for an action, an individual must have had guidance control over the action, which entails the action stemming from the agent's own, moderately reasons-responsive mechanism. This mechanism is shaped by the action's history and involves the capacity to recognise and respond appropriately to moral reasons. According to Fischer and Ravizza, then, it seems that no ex-post declaration could ever change one's responsibility. What counts is how the action or outcome was brought about and, in particular, whether there was relevant control in terms of reason-responsiveness (Fischer and Ravizza 1998).

Alternatively, consider so called quality of will theorists like Shoemaker. According to Shoemaker, we are responsible for conduct, actions, and outcomes when they reflect our quality of will, ie our quality of character, judgement or regard for others. But such reflection of the quality of will can only happen in how some conduct, action or outcome was brought about and not simply be forged by declaration (Shoemaker 2015). Thus, even though Shoemaker and other quality of will theorists have a lot to disagree about with control theorists like Fischer and Ravizza, they still converge on the view that ex-post declarations are irrelevant to a person's responsibility.

The contrast between these orthodox views on responsibility and the notion of a normative power in taking responsibility can vary significantly based on our interpretation of a key metaphysical aspect of responsibility. Specifically, this aspect is whether responsibility is a 'sharp' concept – meaning someone is in a precise way always either fully responsible or not responsible at all, with no intermediate states – or a 'vague' concept, where clear cases exist at both ends but indeterminacy remains in between.

If we assume that responsibility is ontologically (not just epistemically) vague, then taking responsibility represents the transition from a grey area of indeterminate responsibility to a state of clear responsibility. Conversely, if we assume responsibility is ontologically sharp, then taking responsibility would mean transitioning from a state of no responsibility to full responsibility – essentially, from black to white.

Both views can adequately address the *Lorry Driver Paradox*, so I will remain neutral on this point. However, the vagueness view may offer certain advantages. It posits a less radical normative power, thus reducing deviation from the orthodox view, and it avoids the need for additional explanations regarding an otherwise arising asymmetry between the sharpness of responsibility and the previously mentioned vagueness of the penumbra of agency (the 'grey area') on which responsibility supervenes.

TAKING RESPONSIBILITY IN PUBLIC INTERNATIONAL LAW

Let me now proceed to the second comparison, the comparison with the law, in particular state immunity in public international law.

State immunity is a fundamental principle of international law, acting as a procedural barrier that prevents states and their representatives from being sued or prosecuted in foreign courts (Fox and Webb 2015).[3] State immunity facilitates the performance of public functions by shielding states from the adjudicative and enforcement jurisdiction of the courts of the forum state, particularly in specific

[3] See also *Republic of Austria v Altmann*, 541 US 677, 689 (2004); Jasper Finke (2010, 870–871).

classes of cases where a foreign state is involved (Crawford and Brownlie 2019, 470–471).

Immunity has long been recognised as a norm of customary international law. In addition, there are several international treaties and conventions that codify the principles of state immunity, including the United Nations Convention on Jurisdictional Immunities of States and Their Property (2004) (Crawford and Brownlie 2019, 472 ff). But the doctrine's rationale is also deeply rooted in the concept of sovereign equality, encapsulated in the maxim '*par in parem non habet imperium*' – meaning 'an equal has no power over an equal'. This principle emphasises the idea that sovereign entities do not possess the authority to bring other sovereigns before their own courts without consent (Amirfar 2019, 167–169).

But saying that sovereigns cannot be brought to foreign courts *without their consent* already indicates that said consent could make a difference. And indeed, state immunity is not unchangeable; it can be *waived* (State Immunity Act 1978, s 2(7); *Aziz v Republic of Yemen* [2005] EWCA Civ 745, [48]; *Donegal International Ltd v Republic of Zambia* [2007] EWHC 197 (Comm)). In fact, the waiver of state immunity is an important and nuanced concept in international law, allowing a state voluntarily to relinquish its legal protection against being sued or prosecuted in foreign courts. The State Immunity Act 1978 outlines four specific methods for a state to waive its immunity: submission to jurisdiction after a dispute arises; prior written agreement; initiating proceedings; or intervening in proceedings. However, this Act also distinguishes between waiver of immunity from jurisdiction and immunity from execution, emphasising that the former does not automatically entail the latter (Juratowitch 2016; Denza 2016).

The reasons why states may waive their immunity in public international law are multifaceted, they involve a balance between upholding the principles of sovereign equality and immunity, and they address the demands for justice, accountability and adherence to international norms. Admittedly, sometimes, there may simply be pragmatic considerations that play a significant role in a state's decision to waive immunity. This includes situations where the challenges of maintaining immunity, such as strained diplomatic relations or adverse public opinion, outweigh the benefits. In such contexts, waiving immunity can be a practical response to mitigate negative impacts on the state's international standing and to address real-world complications that might arise from rigidly adhering to immunity.

However, there are also two more substantial reasons for states to waive their immunity. First, there is the protection of norms and values. By waiving immunity, a state shows its commitment to upholding international law and norms, particularly in areas such as human rights. This action not only expresses adherence to established norms but also helps preserve the integrity of the principles of immunity. Such a move ensures these principles are not misused or abused, reinforcing the idea that immunity should facilitate international relations and legal fairness, rather than shield states from accountability for serious misconduct.

Second, there is the maintenance and improvement of international relations. The waiver of immunity is also a tool for fostering and developing international relations. It can be seen as a gesture of goodwill, demonstrating a state's dedication to strong, cooperative international relations, and can enhance a state's global reputation as a responsible member of the international community. Moreover, the principle of reciprocity in international relations plays a crucial role; a state's willingness to waive immunity under appropriate circumstances can encourage other states to reciprocate, fostering a culture of mutual respect and trust. This reciprocal approach can greatly benefit diplomatic interactions, promoting international cooperation and contributing to global peace (*cf* Verdier and Voeten 2015).

So understood, waiving immunity, just like immunity itself, is an important part of a state's position in international law. But what is most important for my purposes here is that waiving immunity can be understood as a normative power to take responsibility. By waiving immunity, a state creates responsibility by declaration in a very specific sense: it makes itself answerable to others, or a specific legal forum, when it previously was not answerable. What is more, waiving immunity creates answerability for something in the past, ie it concerns taking retrospective responsibility in the way described earlier. It is therefore no coincidence that some scholars compare this act to another normative power, ie consent. As Jürgen Bröhmer succinctly explains: 'Waiver of immunity is just another term for consenting to submit to the jurisdiction of the forum' (Bröhmer 1997, 191).

But we should also be aware of a crucial difference between waiving immunity and the normative power of taking responsibility as Enoch introduced it: waiving immunity concerns the *removal* of a procedural barrier to one's answerability. It does not concern the *creation* of responsibility. In the context of waiving immunity, it is not that the act was in the penumbra or grey area of the state's agency and then integrated into its agency by taking responsibility. The act under consideration was in the core of a state's agency. It is just that by waiving immunity, and taking responsibility, the state reinstates the standing of others to hold it responsible. So, there are two different ideas: taking responsibility by committing to acts or their consequences in the penumbra or grey are of one's agency, versus taking responsibility by removing a procedural barrier and thereby creating the standing for others to hold one responsible.

Yet, despite this difference, the law outlines how responsibility can be determined by declarations after the fact. We may therefore ask whether we can endorse some aspects of this legal approach and transfer it to the philosophical idea of a normative power to take responsibility. This is what I shall investigate in the next section.

UNITING PHILOSOPHICAL AND LEGAL PERSPECTIVES

The law suggested that waiving immunity can protect and maintain relations. In philosophy, Mason developed a similar idea. Mason talks about 'taking responsibility' and she says: 'there are certain conditions under which we should take responsibility, and that when we do so, we genuinely are responsible' (Mason 2018, 164). Moreover, in taking responsibility, Mason says: 'We … extend the realm of our own responsibility' (Mason 2018, 172–173).

It is important to note important differences to the normative power of taking responsibility featured in this chapter. First, Mason focuses on 'responsibility in the sense of blameworthiness' (Mason 2018, 172). By contrast, my concern is with responsibility in the sense of answerability. Second, Mason makes emotions central. Taking responsibility is 'emotional' (Mason 2018, 177) on her view. Mason says that 'remorse … is essential in taking responsibility' (Mason 2019, 188). By contrast, I do not require any emotional component in the act of taking responsibility. Finally, Mason's view, 'taking on responsibility is more like a disposition' (Mason 2018, 178). By contrast, I consider 'taking responsibility' to be a normative power, normally performed via an explicit speech act.

Nevertheless, what Mason says about her account can be transferred to the normative power of taking responsibility. Mason says that 'the reason for taking on responsibility in certain cases is that it is constitutive of respectful relationships' (Mason 2018, 177), and adds: 'We voluntarily extend our responsibility zone in order to secure the respect and trust of others, and as a way of showing commitment and investment in our relationships' (Mason 2019, 185). Mason's examples concern personal relationships between friends, family members, partners and so on. In such cases, 'taking extended responsibility is sometimes fitting, but it is morally optional. Whether it is a good idea depends on the social context. Sometimes our relationships require it, sometimes they do not' (Mason 2019, 201). On this basis, Mason then claims that 'the lorry driver … has no duty to take on responsibility or blameworthiness … it is not required by the relationship in play' (Mason 2018, 178). The Enoch-style and legally inspired view under consideration can accept Mason's starting point, namely that the development and maintenance of relationships can be an important consideration in taking responsibility, but transcend the boundaries of personal relationships, narrowly conceived, that would exclude the moral relations that someone like the lorry driver could cultivate with those who were harmed.

In addition, the law suggested that waiving immunity can express values and commitment to norms. Wolf may have provided philosophical grounds for this idea, namely by showing how taking responsibility can be an act of virtue. But first, we need to note important differences between Wolf's view and the normative power featured in this chapter. Wolf's main concern is also with blame and blameworthiness, rather than answerability. Moreover, Wolf's proposal holds that taking responsibility does not change the objective facts about the lorry driver's responsibility, but only permits a certain self-directed response, ie a different sense of holding *oneself* responsible. By contrast, Enoch and I argue that taking responsibility makes a difference to the driver's responsibility too and how others may now react to him. In other words, Wolf presents an explanation of the inner moral psychology of the lucky and unlucky driver, whereas I focus on the outer responsibility.

Yet, Wolf's discussion is insightful for the normative power of taking responsibility too. In particular, Wolf argues that taking responsibility for one's actions and their consequences is a virtuous act, akin to generosity, because it often involves going beyond justice or obligation to benefit others, even at a personal cost. This virtue involves a willingness to be held accountable and to make amends, potentially even paying for damages or apologising for unintended harm. In her words:

> There is a virtue that I suspect we all dimly recognize and commend that may be expressed as the virtue of taking responsibility for one's actions and their consequences. It is, regrettably, a virtue with no name, and I am at a loss to suggest a name that would be helpful. It involves living with an expectation and a willingness to be held accountable for what one does, understanding the scope of 'what one does,' particularly when costs are involved, in an expansive rather than a narrow way. It is the virtue that would lead one to offer to pay for the vase that one broke even if one's fault in the incident was uncertain; the virtue that would lead one to apologize, rather than get defensive, if one unwittingly offended someone or hurt him. Perhaps this virtue is a piece or an aspect of a larger one which involves taking responsibility not just for one's actions and their consequences, but for a larger range of circumstances that fall broadly within one's reach. One may offer to pay for the vase one's child broke, or offer to take the blame for the harm someone suffered as a result of the practices of an agency of which one is the head. (Wolf 2001, 13)

> Perhaps the more obvious reason for regarding it as a virtue is that, when applied to harmful actions, this trait is a species of, or at least akin to, the well-established virtue of generosity. Generosity generally involves a willingness to give more – more time, more money, more love, more lenience, more, in one way or another, of oneself than justice requires. … an agent voluntarily benefits or tries to benefit others at cost to herself. That this should be seen as virtuous is not hard to understand. (Wolf 2001, 14)

However, as Wolf hastens to add, 'the virtue … is not so clearly or narrowly moral' (Wolf 2001, 14). It also concerns how we view ourselves. Wolf argues that seeing oneself as separate from the effects one has on the world is unhealthy and undesirable. She believes the value of taking responsibility lies in acknowledging our interconnectedness with others and the world, recognising that our actions significantly impact who we are and what we should do. For this reason, taking responsibility is a key component of our self-conception of 'creatures of a physical and social world' (Wolf 2001, 18) and that we 'are beings who are thoroughly in-the-world, in interaction with others whose movements and thoughts we cannot fully control' (Wolf 2001, 14).[4]

Thus, to come full circle: the law's two suggestions about waiving immunity, ie that it can maintain and develop relationship and that it expresses values and commitment to norms, can be philosophically supported and applied to the normative power of taking responsibility. This shows an opportunity to link two rather separate fields of inquiry: although neither quite captured the idea of normative power of taking responsibility, we can use their synergy to develop exactly this idea of a normative power and thus provide a distinctive solution to the *Lorry Driver Paradox*. On this basis, the lorry driver's decision to take responsibility for the accident can be understood through the perspectives of Mason and Wolf, as well as being reflected in the law on waiving immunity. Mason emphasises that taking responsibility fosters respectful relationships; by extending his responsibility zone, the lorry driver demonstrates a commitment to honouring his relationships with his victims as moral equals. Wolf highlights that taking responsibility is a virtuous act; and accordingly, the lorry driver's willingness to accept accountability shows he is less concerned with saving his own face than addressing the harm he caused to others. These considerations then inform our analysis of when the lorry driver *ought* to take responsibility, that is when the act of taking responsibility realises the values highlighted by Wolf, Mason and public international law, and they thus complement my earlier analysis (regarding the two conditions) of when the driver *can* take responsibility.

TWO OBJECTIONS

Now that the idea of a normative power of 'taking responsibility' is laid out, I shall address two fundamental objections to Enoch's version of this normative

[4] Enoch explicitly built on Wolf's ideas in his own account too. Enoch argues that the normative power to take responsibility is essential for maintaining a healthy self-conception as agents, whose actions have real-world consequences beyond mere intentions. Specifically, Enoch claims that 'there is value in … the power to take responsibility for the consequences of our actions [because it] seems necessary for our ability to think of ourselves as such impure agents' (Enoch 2012, 124). Impure agents are those whose agency is not 'utterly independent of the consequences our intentions (and the like) have in the real world' (Enoch 2012, 124) and who accept the consequences of their actions as integral to their agency. In fact, Enoch repeatedly says that 'we should take interest in the world, not just in our will or intention' (Enoch 2012, 127), that 'we should think of ourselves as creatures whose intentions and bodily movements have effects in the world' (Enoch 2012, 127), and that, therefore, 'we have … reason to incorporate the unintended and unforeseen consequences of our actions into our agency' (Enoch 2012, 127). The 'should' or 'reason' in these quotations oscillates between a more deontic sense of 'morally required' and a more axiological sense of being useful for our self-conception and thriving in our world as it is.

power of taking responsibility and argue that we need to make two equally fundamental modifications. This will lead me to my own approach on taking responsibility, which also solves the *Lorry Driver Paradox* but departs from Enoch's view in important respects.

Objection 1: The Power-Duty Nexus

It is widely held that we possess a certain normative power only if that power has some positive value for us, ie only if it is good or desirable in some sense that we have that power.[5] Traditionally, philosophers explained this value in terms of how certain normative powers promote our autonomy (Hurd 1996; Shiffrin 2008; Watson 2009; Westlund 2013) or help us to establish important relationships (Enoch 2012; Owens 2012; Bennett 2018).

On any of these conceptions, however, the value of a normative power crucially depends on whether one has sufficient moral discretion over the exercise of it. For instance, the value of consent for our autonomy, be it medical consent or sexual consent, crucially depends on the fact that we could normally say 'no' and refuse to consent without acting wrongly. After all, it must be up to us what to decide. If we were morally obliged to consent whenever consenting was an option, the value of consent for our autonomy would be eliminated altogether. A similar picture arises for promising. When we make promises, David Owens argues, we build valuable relationships. Seana Shiffrin adds that we thereby also balance power asymmetries. But the value that promising has, both for oneself and for others, depends on our usual freedom to give or withhold a promise. In fact, the very idea of promising is premised on the thought that we ought to have some genuine discretion over our obligations.[6]

[5] Generally, the value of a normative power concerns the value for the person possessing it and this will be my main focus too. However, in some conceptions of normative powers, especially in legal contexts, the value of a normative power may mainly concern the value it has for others. See, for instance, Joseph Raz's service conception of authority (see Raz 2009). Moreover, note that I state only a necessary condition here, not a sufficient one: ie that the value of a normative power is necessary but not sufficient for its existence. Some other authors, however, also endorsed a sufficient condition (see for instance Raz 1999, 69–73; 2019). Discussed in Ulrike Heuer (2012a, 2012b).

[6] The significance of moral discretion has also been emphasised beyond the debate on normative powers. General accounts of autonomy and freedom have stressed the significance of moral discretion too. For instance, Raz says: 'Autonomy requires that … morally acceptable options be available to a person', and he explains that this requires 'a choice of goods. A choice between good and evil is not enough' (Raz 1986, 378, 379). If a person can only pick one option if she is to be moral, then that person does not enjoy valuable autonomy. Victor Tadros made a similar point when he said that 'Certain actions are not valuable as free expressions of agency because of the significance of the reasons against acting in that way. Respect for these values makes valuing one's free performance of such actions inappropriate' (Tadros 2016, 44). Thus, moral discretion is crucial to autonomy and valuable freedom more generally.

Unfortunately, Enoch seems to exclude such discretion. As stated before, Enoch claimed that the lorry driver is not only *able* to take responsibility, but also that he is *obliged* to do so. In fact, none of Enoch's cases allows for any moral discretion. The protagonists in Enoch's examples are always under a moral duty to take responsibility. I shall call this feature Enoch's *power-duty nexus*.

The *power-duty nexus* creates a fundamental problem as it turns *any* act of not taking responsibility into an act of wrongdoing.[7] But if so, the apparently attractive freedom over determining one's own responsibility that Enoch's normative power provides has great *instrumental disvalue*, by which I mean that making use of it and thereby avoiding responsibility leads to something undesirable. It leads to moral wrongdoing, it is likely to incur justified social censure and blame, it creates morally stained relationships with those we wrong by avoiding responsibility (eg the lorry driver wronging the child's parents), and it damages our lives for these reasons. But if so, one widely accepted strategy in supporting the existence of a normative power, namely one based on the value of moral discretion, does not apply to Enoch's view.[8]

However, one may object at this point and try to rescue Enoch's view by pointing to John Milton's *Paradise Lost*. Milton reports God as saying about men: 'I made [them] just and right, sufficient to have stood, *though free to fall*' (Milton 2014, book 3: v98–99; emphasis added). The freedom to fall is the freedom to act wrongly. Such freedom may have great instrumental disvalue too. Yet, or so an interpretation goes, it also has intrinsic and all-things-considered positive value because such freedom to fall is a pre-condition of free moral agency. If men were compelled to do the right thing, they would not qualify as free moral agents and lose out on an important value in human life. Milton's verse has created a philosophical legacy. Philosophers in the debate on moral enhancement (*cf* J Harris 2011) as well as those in the philosophy of religion (*cf* Hasker 2000) have argued in a similar way that the general freedom to act wrongly, despite its instrumental disvalue, is a pre-condition of free moral agency and, therefore, valuable, all things considered. Thus, could Enoch equally concede the instrumental disvalue of avoiding responsibility but still insist that it is valuable, all things considered?

Unfortunately, Milton's line of reasoning cannot help Enoch's view. Milton and others focused on the *very possibility* to act wrongly, as only this is a precondition of free moral agency and thereby acquires the intrinsic value that

[7] To clarify: Not every instance of failing to fulfil an obligation qualifies as wrongdoing, because obligations can be overridden. Thus, my critique of Enoch's position comes with a qualification: *where there are no other overriding considerations*, any act of not taking responsibility is an act of wrongdoing.

[8] Note that I still claim that only the normative power requires a value-based explanation, not that the duty requires such an explanation.

Milton and others saw in it. By contrast, the *one* additional option of wrongdoing that Enoch's obligatory act of taking responsibility creates is not in any way required for our status as free moral agents. Hence, the case against Enoch's normative power still stands.

But a second rejoinder could point out that Enoch never subscribed to an absolute power-duty nexus. He only said that there is a duty in 'the cases of taking responsibility *of the kind I'm interested in*' (Enoch 2012, 107, emphasis added). But this is consistent with leaving open the possibility that there are many *other* cases in which the duty to take responsibility does *not* arise. Accordingly, the duty to exercise the normative power of taking responsibility could just concern one type of case, just as the occasional duty to give a promise does. Let us assume that this is Enoch's position, or at least the most charitable interpretation of it. Yet, even then, his view remains unsatisfactory for three reasons.

First, it remains *incomplete*. Enoch only elaborates on cases in which taking responsibility is obligatory and never mentions a case in which it is subject to moral discretion. But if moral discretion is key to the justification of a normative power, Enoch has not addressed one of the most important aspects of the justification of a normative power.

Second, Enoch's view risks being *circular*. As mentioned before, Enoch says little about why exactly the driver is under a duty to take responsibility. But it seems that any reasons for such a duty come dangerously close to, or could even be understood as, reasons as to why the driver *is* already responsible in some sense. For instance, taking responsibility, considered as a directed duty owed to the victim, could stem from the fact that there already is some (equally directed) responsibility owed to the victim. But if so, the possibility of taking responsibility would at least be partly explained by some pre-existing responsibility and thus render Enoch's proposal circular, and even self-defeating. But to be clear: this is not to say that Enoch could not in principle find a way to avoid such circularity. It is only to say that, in the absence of a more elaborate explanation of the duty to take responsibility, this remains a weakness in his account.

Third, and most importantly, Enoch's emphasis on the duty to take responsibility is *redundant*, by which I mean that we do not need it to solve the *Lorry Driver Paradox* and support the existence of the normative power of taking responsibility. Recall claim (3) of *The Lorry Driver Paradox:* the driver $ought_1$ to take responsibility and, having done so, subsequently also $ought_2$ to give a genuine apology for the child's death. The first 'ought', $ought_1$, could be understood as an aretaic (virtue-related) 'ought', referring to something that is supererogatory rather than obligatory (as Enoch would have it). The second 'ought', $ought_2$, however, could still be understood as a deontic (obligation-related) 'ought', since taking responsibility makes it *then* obligatory for a person also to follow through and, eg, apologise. And note: such a combination of a virtue-related and an obligation-related ought is not unusual. In fact, such cases are familiar in the context of promising; the *making* of a promise (ie that one 'ought' to promise some particular action) may be a supererogatory act of virtue, while the *keeping* of that promise (ie that one 'ought' to do as promised) remains a deontic, ie obligatory, requirement. On this basis, we can still solve the inconsistency in the *Lorry Driver Paradox* without subscribing to the view that there is a duty to take responsibility. We thereby avoid the *power-duty nexus* that jars with how normative powers are often justified. Thus, the power-duty nexus is a disposable feature in the kind of argument that I propose.

What is more, once we abandon the power-duty nexus, not taking responsibility would no longer be a wrong, the instrumental disvalue of the freedom not to take responsibility is eliminated or at least greatly reduced, and genuine moral discretion arises once more. At the same time, this is compatible with saying that the lorry driver's taking responsibility is still an act of virtue and therefore favoured by (potentially strong) *moral* reasons, even if these reasons do not constitute obligations. Furthermore, once we shift our focus to supererogation, the act of taking responsibility could also be a more laudable achievement, as people would thereby do what lies beyond what others could reasonably demand. And the opportunity for such an achievement could figure in an explanation as to why it would be very valuable to have this normative power, namely because this power creates an opportunity for moral excellence. Hence, my proposal would then be to relinquish Enoch's power-duty nexus and explain the act of taking responsibility in terms of supererogation rather than obligation.

Objection 2: No Genuine Moral Answerability

I claimed (in agreement with Enoch) that, initially, the lorry driver was not morally answerable for the accident. Answerability theorists will happily agree and even offer an explanation. For instance, Angela Smith argues that '[i]n order for an agent to be answerable for something, … the thing in question must in some way reflect her own judgment or assessment of reasons' (Angela Smith 2015, 103). Yet, the accident did not reflect the driver's judgement or assessment of reasons. It was just bad luck.

Later, however, I added (still in agreement with Enoch) that the driver can *become* morally answerable for the accident, namely by taking responsibility. But at this point, answerability theorists must balk. The act of taking responsibility cannot magically make it the case that the accident now reflects the driver's judgement when previously it did not. And if the act of taking responsibility cannot create a reflection of judgement, it cannot create answerability. Thus, creating answerability at will is impossible. The answerability theorists may concede that, after 'taking responsibility', the driver could be legitimately addressed in some way (ie grant 'addressability'), but add that he still lacks genuine morally responsibility (ie deny 'answerability').[9]

What is more, the answerability theorists could further substantiate this objection by pointing to the work of a lawyer. When taking on a new client, a lawyer makes herself an appropriate addressee of claims concerning her client. It has now become her professional responsibility to answer for the client in the sense of being obliged to provide an explanation of the client's conduct in court (within certain limits). Yet, the lawyer does not thereby become morally responsible for what the client did or does. So, being obliged to provide an explanation or justification is not enough for possessing moral answerability. Thus, the kind of 'responsibility' that the lorry driver takes might be similar to the kind of 'addressability' that lawyers take when accepting new clients but still fall short of genuine moral responsibility.

This important objection forces a proponent of the normative taking of responsibility to reply in one of the following two ways:

(i) Taking responsibility *does* forge the link required for moral answerability, ie it makes it the case that the accident reflects the driver's quality of judgement.
(ii) Moral answerability does not require a reflection of judgement and, hence, the driver can be genuinely morally responsible even if the accident does not reflect his judgement.

Option (i) is implausible. It is very unclear, to say the least, how the act of taking responsibility could connect the driver's judgements to the accident in such a way that the accident now morally reflects on the driver when it did *not* do so before. However, the more fundamental problem with this response is that, *even if* taking responsibility could forge the required link, it would follow that taking responsibility is no longer a genuine normative power.

When exercising a normative power, a person *directly* changes the normative landscape, eg by a simple declaration or performance of a mental act, rather than by changing the world so that the change occurs *indirectly* (*cf* Tadros 2020a). For instance, when I unjustifiably hit someone, I incur an obligation to apologise. But hitting someone is not an exercise of normative power that creates an obligation because I do not directly impose an obligation on myself by my will or

[9] This line of reasoning resembles David Hume's concerns about the possibility of normative powers. Hume argued that a mere declaration could not change reasons as it could not change interests on which reasons depend. The objection under consideration here claims, similarly, that a mere declaration could not forge a reflection of judgement and hence cannot create answerability. *cf* Jed Lewinsohn (2024).

declaration, as I would do when, say, 'I promise to do X'; instead I am only indirectly imposing an obligation on myself by performing a separate act that causes a change in the world. Thus, something is a normative power in the robust sense only if it is my will or declaration that causes the change in the normative landscape. As Ruth Chang notes: 'Genuine normative powers create reasons in a way that is distinct from the way in which reasons are typically generated by happenings in the world …: when we exercise a normative power, we will that things be thus and so, by way of that very willing …, [and] not by way of some other state in the world' (Chang 2020, 276–277).

Building on these thoughts, it then follows that if taking responsibility creates the 'reflection of judgement', which in turn leads to moral answerability, the act of taking responsibility is not a normative power for the same reason that hitting someone is not. Thus, option (i) ought to be rejected.

Option (ii) is what remains, but is there a possibility that one is or, more specifically, *becomes* morally responsible for something even if this something does not reflect one's quality of will? At this point, looking at the law might help. In the law, there can be responsibility as answerability without reflection of judgement, namely in those cases where answerability is made 'strict', as explained in the previous chapter. To recall, answerability is strict when, solely by virtue of having performed a certain act (*actus reus*), and regardless of mental state (*mens rea*) like intention, recklessness, or negligence, a person can be summoned to answer in court. For instance, if someone sells contaminated food, they can be charged with the offence of '[s]elling food not of the nature or substance or quality demanded', under s 14 of the Food Safety Act 1990. Yet, at this point, they do not yet incur liability because s 21(1) also states that it is 'a defence for the person charged to prove that he took all reasonable precautions and exercised all due diligence to avoid the commission of the offence'. Thus, this is not a case of the better-known strict *liability*, but only a case of strict *answerability*.

In these latter cases, including selling adulterated food, the action does not need to reflect the person's judgement for them to be answerable in court. Nevertheless, the law considers it a genuine form of responsibility. Moreover, some legal theorists have argued that strict answerability is not just a legal peculiarity but also extends to morality. In fact, Duff argued that moral answerability is even *typically* strict in morality: 'in moral contexts answerability is typically strict: I must answer morally for the harms that I cause even if I cause them through non-culpable accident or inadvertence' (Duff 2009b, 893–984; *cf* Duff 2009a, 220, 230).

For the purposes of this chapter and the objection under consideration, I shall leave aside what the various *conditions* might be for a person to become strictly morally or legally answerable. Instead, I shall focus on the *idea* of strict answerability itself as it claims that there can be answerability without reflection of judgement. Moreover, it spells out answerability in terms of an obligation to explain one's conduct. And for this reason, it aligns more closely with the normative power of taking responsibility.

This form of (strict) answerability is also importantly different from the 'addressability' of the lawyer. The strictly answerable person may face personal liability (moral or legal) when they cannot provide an adequate explanation (ie excuse or justification) of their conduct, whereas the addressable lawyer does not face any such liability. Thus, there is a path from strict answerability to liability, but not from addressability to liability. And this connection suggests that strict answerability is unlike addressability and, instead, is a form of genuine responsibility.

But even if we concede that strict answerability is genuine responsibility, the type of answerability that one can 'take' via a normative power is significantly different from that which moral philosophers describe. For this reason, defending the idea of taking responsibility as a normative power ultimately implies a commitment to another form of answerability and cannot, as Enoch suggests, just rely on the common conception of answerability. This is, then, the second important modification of Enoch's view that we need to accept in order to defend the idea of taking responsibility. *Pace* Enoch, we cannot simply rely on the orthodox understanding of moral answerability in the philosophical literature, but rather must take some further inspiration from the law. On the one hand, this creates another challenge, namely a debate about whether strict answerability could, in fact, be genuine moral answerability, as Duff suggests (Duff 2009b, 893–984; *cf* Duff 2009a, 220, 230) and Shoemaker denies (Shoemaker 2013, 164). On the other hand, it creates an opportunity to bring together legal and philosophical scholarship on responsibility and explore a dimension of responsibility that moral philosophers have given short shrift to. The view I propose holds that some form of strict answerability, ie answerability without reflection of judgement, can be genuine moral responsibility and, on this basis, my view differs from Enoch's view in a significant way.

CONCLUSION

The motivation for this chapter, like the previous one, was a novel puzzle concerning responsibility, which I called the *Lorry Driver Paradox*, and it developed the idea of a normative power of taking responsibility to solve it. In so doing, I supported the normative power of taking responsibility as a solution to a specific puzzle, rather than, as Enoch did, as a device to capture the moral phenomenology of different cases. Moreover, unlike Enoch, I argued that the normative power of taking responsibility needs to be separated from what I called a power-duty nexus, and that it requires an approach to answerability which differs from the philosophical orthodoxy. I suggested that this investigation of a normative power to take responsibility can benefit from a comparison to the waiver of state immunity in international public law and the acknowledgment of strict answerability, as it arises in the context of reverse burdens of proof. This gives us a second feasible solution to the *Lorry Driver Paradox* and reinforces the significance of legal scholarship in advancing our understanding of moral responsibility.

4

Pascal's Apology

IN THIS CHAPTER, I shall discuss a third and final potential solution to the *Lorry Driver Paradox*, based on the idea of what I call *Pascal's Apology*.[1] This solution takes inspiration from *Pascal's Wager*, which I explore more fully below but briefly state here: it is a philosophical argument which holds that when one faces uncertainty about a situation, it is safest to choose the course of action with the least potential downside and the greatest potential moral benefit. Applied to the lorry driver, this approach stresses that the driver could never be certain as to whether he was in some way negligent, and argues that apologising is the morally safest choice for the driver. So, like *Pascal's Wager*, there is the *Lorry Driver's Wager*: it is better to apologise even if one turns out not to be responsible, rather than not apologise when one was, in fact, in some way responsible. This solution will introduce modal qualifiers, stating – in (1) – that the driver is *likely* not morally responsible and – in (2) – that one ought to apologise only if one is *possibly* morally responsible. And with these qualifications, the inconsistency disappears. But this chapter will also further illuminate the reasons the driver may have for apologising and provide a more in-depth examination of the relationship between answerability, culpability, and apology. To do so, I shall first present the solution of *Pascal's Apology* in greater detail before discussing its defence and implications.

OUTLINE OF THE SOLUTION: *PASCAL'S APOLOGY*

The solution of *Pascal's Apology* does not fully reject any of the three premises outright, but rather proposes a modification of them. Its central idea is that the *Lorry Driver Paradox* emerges only under idealised conditions of perfect knowledge, which are far removed from our real-world moral experiences. In real-life scenarios, like that of a lorry driver, certainty about moral responsibility or the appropriateness of an apology is elusive. Considering this, we can refine the initially inconsistent triad by adding just two words (emphasised in bold):

(1) The faultless driver is ***likely*** not morally responsible for the child's death.

[1] I owe this term to Simon Kirchin, who suggested it to me in discussion of my proposal.

(2) *Apology Principle:* one ought to apologise for something only if one is ***possibly*** morally responsible for it.
(3) The driver ought to apologise for the child's death.

The two words are modal qualifiers (ie 'likely' and 'possibly'), and they suffice to remove the inconsistency. The *likelihood* of *not* being responsible is consistent with the *possibility* of *being* responsible. But this solution still raises the question as to why the driver ought to apologise in this situation of uncertainty. After all, the *Apology Principle* only states a necessary but not sufficient condition of an apology. In this context, therefore, a possible solution may not only resolve the inconsistency within the triad of claims but also provide a further explanation as to why the driver ought to apologise.

A possible explanation is what I term *Pascal's Apology*, paralleling *Pascal's Wager*. Blaise Pascal argued that the uncertainty about God's existence should guide our belief. If God exists and one disbelieves, the consequences are potentially severe, eg eternal punishment. However, if God doesn't exist and one still believes, the loss is minimal. Therefore, Pascal reasoned, belief in God is the safer bet regardless of the truth. Similarly, in the context of the lorry driver, the rationale would be that apologising, despite uncertainty, is a safer moral choice. David Sussman, although without referring to Pascal, explains how:

> If nothing else, he [ie the driver] should realize that it would be much worse to actually be at fault and fail to acknowledge it, apologize, or make some reparative gesture than to make these gestures when they turned out not to be needed. To deny people what they are owed is an injustice; to give them more than they deserve is usually an unobjectionable kindness. (Sussman 2018, 800)

Sussman captures the essence of the proposed solution in this chapter, but I need to go further and specify the proposal under consideration, especially by contrasting it with two interpretations and aligning it with a third.

First, the proposed solution is not an 'if' model, in the sense that the driver would say 'I apologise *if* I am responsible', thereby not yet giving an actual apology, but rather making something like a promise to apologise (later) if he turns out to be responsible. In the case at hand, I assume that the driver gives an actual apology.

Second, the proposed solution is also not an 'as-if' model either, in the sense that the driver would pretend to be responsible and then apologise. The driver mentions the uncertainty about his responsibility to avoid giving the false impression to others that he may be genuinely responsible or even culpable. The driver does not gloss over or cover up the uncertainty, nor does he entertain any illusion about his responsibility. He suspends judgment.

The interpretation of the driver's apology is best captured by the 'in-case' model, in the sense that the driver apologises in case he is responsible. There is a subtle difference between 'if' phrases and 'in case' phrases. To say that I will take my umbrella *if* it rains means that rain is a condition for my taking the umbrella, and that I will not take it unless there is precipitation. To say that I will take my umbrella *in case* it rains means that I will take my umbrella now as a precautionary measure for the possibility that it will rain later. In this latter case, actually taking my umbrella does not have precursory rain as a condition. Similarly with the driver, actually apologising does not have (the proof of) responsibility as a condition, as it would in the 'if model'.

In one important sense, the 'in case' model is not an instance of a conditional apology: the apology is given and not conditional on anything else. Yet, in another sense, there is a conditional element, namely that the apology is voidable on the condition that there is no responsibility. In other words, the continued standing or validity of the apology depends on the evidence of responsibility. Should it later turn out that the driver was not responsible, he can retract the apology and those who received it have reasons, or maybe even an obligation, to withdraw their previous acceptance of it.

So understood, *Pascal's Apology* differs from Peter Baumann's seemingly similar account of conditional apologies in two respects. Baumann writes:

> If S did do X but is uncertain whether they did it or not, then 'If I Xed, I apologize!' constitutes an apology; If S did not do X but is uncertain whether they did it or not, then 'If I Xed, I apologize!' also constitutes an apology but a void one. (Baumann 2021, 1086)

To begin with, unlike Baumann, I do not assume that the apology is *void*, but only *voidable*. In legal terms, 'void' means something is invalid from the start and has no legal or other normative effect, while 'voidable' refers to something that is initially valid but can be cancelled or invalidated later based on certain conditions. Accordingly, my view contrasts with Baumann's in that Baumann considers the apology as 'void' or invalid from the beginning if the necessary conditions are not met. In contrast, I view the apology as 'voidable', meaning it is initially valid but can later be retracted if new evidence shows that the conditions for a genuine apology were not met.

Additionally, my approach in *Pascal's Apology* differs from Baumann's in the specific condition we focus on. While Baumann's view centres on causation and agency – whether the driver actually caused the accident or was the person who ran over the child – my approach emphasises the condition of responsibility. In the case of the lorry driver, there is no denial of causing the accident or being the individual involved. Instead, my focus is on the driver's moral responsibility or culpability, which is the uncertain element in this scenario.

On this reading of an 'in case' apology, the driver gives an actual apology, unlike in the 'if' model, but also one that can be voided. And the driver makes transparent rather than conceals, as in the 'as if' model, that there is genuine epistemic uncertainty about the situation. Yet, and this may be an important difference to Pascal's original wager: the driver is not primarily concerned with his own prudential interests, eg avoiding eternal damnation (as in the original wager) or unpleasant consequences (as in the accident case), but instead has genuine moral concerns about how to avoid offending or wronging others.

So understood, *Pascal's Apology* seems to be an attractive solution for several reasons. First, it solves the inconsistency with a simple pair of modal qualifiers. Thus, it is a parsimonious solution that still allows us to retain much of what we may have found initially plausible in the *Lorry Driver Paradox*. Second, it emphasises a realistic rather than idealised scenario of our moral practice, addressing and not avoiding the inevitable uncertainty we face. For this reason, it is a practice-oriented solution. Third, although it is in some sense a form of a conditional apology, it avoids the usual criticism against such an apology. Conditional apologies are criticised for various reasons[2] and Kristie Miller mentions a key one:

> One reason why conditional retrospective apologies have a bad name is because they are often thought to be used deceptively to both garner the good will and positive benefits of a full and meaningful apology, whilst simultaneously minimising the moral culpability of the author of the apology by falsely alleging that the author of the apology does not know whether the relevant act was one for which he was morally culpable. (Miller 2014, 411–412)

But this critique does not apply to the lorry driver, at least not in the version I specified. There is genuine uncertainty about his culpability and there are no intentions on the driver's part to minimise or conceal his culpability.[3]

ASSESSING *PASCAL'S APOLOGY*

With this description of the solution at hand, I shall now concentrate on what would be required to support it, namely a defence against two challenges which concern premises (2) and (3) of the *Lorry Driver Paradox*.

The proposed solution relies on (2) the *Apology Principle*, at least in the modified version that still stresses a connection between a genuine apology and moral responsibility. But once the Pascalian driver starts to think strategically about the positive consequences of offering an apology (ie precluding potential further offence), one may argue that the solution did not go far enough and claim that an apology should be given irrespective of moral responsibility since it might have very beneficial consequences even in the absence of responsibility too.

[2] See Gill (2000, 13), Lazare (2004, 13, 55–58), N Smith (2008, 60). See also Baumann (2021).

[3] The driver is therefore also very much unlike the so-called 'strategic' apologiser who apologises 'not because she believed that she had committed a moral error but because she sought a strategic advantage' (N Smith 2008, 91), eg in divorce proceedings. The driver clearly does not share the self-interested, strategic rationale of such a spouse.

Thus, defending the solution of *Pascal's Apology* requires the defence of the *Apology Principle* in its modified version.

Moreover, *Pascal's Apology* relies on the possibility of fault. If fault is ruled out, as it may be under conditions of perfect knowledge, *Pascal's Apology* denies premise (3), viz it denies that the driver ought to apologise. As such, *Pascal's Apology* eventually sides with fault-based accounts of apology. I shall discuss whether omitting to apologise under conditions of perfect knowledge is appropriate. If not, *Pascal's Apology* implies an incorrect view, and its reliance on the possibility of fault becomes an erroneous workaround.

To assess these aspects, I shall now investigate claims (2) and (3) of the *Lorry Driver Paradox*, and ask if the solution from *Pascal's Apology* can withstand the scrutiny of the results. I shall argue that *Pascal's Apology* can be defended against the first challenge (concerning premise (2)) but not the second (concerning premise (3)). The result is that the *Lorry Driver Paradox* is reinforced, and the reconsideration of responsibility remains the only feasible way to solve it. (It is also worth noting that this discussion is highly relevant to chapter two and the solution based on strict moral answerability, as that approach relied on a version of the *Apology Principle* which framed responsibility in terms of answerability rather than fault or culpability. Therefore, if it emerges that culpability is indeed required to uphold the *Apology Principle*, the viability of the solution based on strict moral answerability would be undermined.)

Rejection of (2): The *Apology Principle*

The *Apology Principle* is widely accepted. Representative statements include:

> [A] speaker is apologizing to his hearer for something … only if in saying what he does he is accepting responsibility for it. (Kort 1975, 79)
>
> Minimally, to be meaningful, an apology must express regret for the occurrence of a harmful event and acknowledge responsibility for it. (Shuman 2000, 185)
>
> [I]f I were to express something like an apology, and yet go on to … deny responsibility for what happened, … then I may well be making excuses, offering sympathy, crowing, or confessing, but I am not apologising. (MacLachlan 2018, 362)

These statements are stronger than the position that the Pascalian driver endorses. The driver does not 'accept' or 'acknowledge' his responsibility as a moral fact, but only leaves it open as a possibility or hypothesis. Yet, as the scholars maintain, the Pascalian driver still accepts the important connection between responsibility and apology, thereby weakening the *Apology Principle* only with a modal qualifier. For this reason, the driver and these scholars are united against, but are also equally challenged by, those who aim to disconnect apology and responsibility altogether. And it is this disconnection that I shall address.

Consider the following scenario, suggested to me by Susan Wolf.[4] Suppose I am expected at a formal occasion, but on my way I am caught in an unexpected rain shower. When I arrive, soaked to the bone, it seems appropriate that I apologise for my dishevelled appearance. Yet, so Wolf suggests, the weather was beyond my control, and I am not responsible for the situation. If correct, this shows that the *Apology Principle*, according to which one ought to apologise for something only if one is responsible for it, is false: there are occasions when one ought to offer a genuine apology, even if one is not responsible for that which one apologises for.

Wolf's example, while thought-provoking, invites contention. A defender of the *Apology Principle* might challenge the example by questioning both the absence of responsibility and the nature of the apology, offering two possible rebuttals. First, through *modus ponens* the proponent could argue that if one offers a genuine apology, then responsibility must exist too. This viewpoint considers the obligation to maintain a certain decorum at formal events. Even when unforeseen events, like a rain shower, disrupt this, it does not necessarily negate one's responsibility, particularly in terms of answerability. It may only help to avert blame and culpability. Alternatively, the defender might employ *modus tollens*, asserting that if there is no responsibility, then what is offered cannot be a genuine apology, but rather just an expression of regret for one's appearance. After all, it is not clear that saying 'sorry' in Wolf's example means a genuine apology or just the expression of regret. This perspective upholds the *Apology Principle* by challenging the simultaneous presence of a genuine apology and a lack of responsibility. Both responses align with the *Apology Principle* and effectively question the dual aspects of Wolf's scenario: the apology and the absence of responsibility. As a result, instead of unequivocally refuting the *Apology Principle*, Wolf's example leads to an intuitive impasse, suggesting the issue is more complex than initially assumed.

However, advocates of the *Apology Principle* might not be content with merely highlighting an intuitive impasse in Wolf's argument. They could further challenge Wolf by asking her to defend an alternative view. After all, when dismissing responsibility as a necessary condition of a genuine apology, Wolf (and others) still implicitly rely on an alternative necessary condition of an apology, and something like agential or causal involvement might be the most plausible candidate. Otherwise, they would not be able to explain why it is inappropriate for one to apologise for the unkempt appearance of a stranger with whom one had no involvement or connection. An apology in such a case, where one has no agential link to the situation, could be seen as inappropriate or even offensive. Thus, the question arises whether this alternative necessary condition of a genuine apology is superior to responsibility. In what

[4] Wolf suggested this example at the 2021 Roots of Responsibility Workshop 'Responsibility and Control'.

follows, I shall argue that it is not, and thus Wolf's challenge to the *Apology Principle* fails.

Two key criteria emerge for evaluating a necessary condition for an apology. The first criterion involves maintaining a clear distinction between an apology and mere regret. This distinction was emphasised by Paul Davis: 'A genuine apology involves substantially more than regret' (Davis 2002, 169) (cf Helmreich 2015). The second criterion focuses on elucidating the second-personal aspect of apologies, emphasising that apologies are owed to specific individuals. Thus, any proposed necessary condition for an apology needs to address these two key aspects successfully: maintaining a clear distinction from mere regret and explicating the second-personal characteristic of apologies. So, does agential involvement or responsibility present the more plausible view?

I argue that responsibility is the better necessary condition for an apology than agential involvement. To begin with, agential involvement tends to blur the line between apology and regret. Such involvement is generally sufficient to make expressions of regret fitting, but it does not inherently carry the deeper meaning that characterises an apology. The *Apology Principle*, which ties apologies to responsibility, maintains this distinction more effectively. The sets of situations warranting apologies and those warranting agent-regret should not completely overlap, yet with agential involvement as the criterion, they are at risk of doing so.

Moreover, regarding the second-personal nature of apologies, responsibility aligns more closely with this aspect than agential involvement. Responsibility is inherently second-personal; it is not only about being responsible *for something* but also about being responsible *to* some*one*. This relational aspect is central to the concept of responsibility. Therefore, when responsibility is posited as a condition for apology, it naturally extends its second-personal character to the apology itself. Apologies, under this framework, inherit their second-personal nature from the responsibility underlying them. Agential (or causal) involvement, on the other hand, lacks this inherently relational dimension, making it less capable of explaining why apologies are owed to specific others.

However, those critiquing the *Apology Principle* might object and assert that agential or causal involvement in causing harm is also always directed towards someone and thus sufficiently accounts for the second-personal nature of apologies. However, this line of reasoning is inadequate. Apologies are not necessarily owed to the person who suffered harm, but are instead, owed to the individual towards whom there was, or is, an obligation or responsibility.

HLA Hart's example can elucidate this point. Hart explains that, in the context of a promise, the notions of rights and obligations diverge from the idea of benefiting from the performance of an obligation. For instance, if X promises Y to care for his mother in exchange for a favour, it is Y, not the mother, who holds the rights emerging from this agreement. Y's mother may benefit from X's obligation, and suffer if it is neglected, but it is to Y that X owes the obligation to care. Thus, if X fails to fulfil the promise, it is Y who is wronged and to whom an apology is owed, regardless of the mother's possible suffering. Y has the moral claim and the right to waive it, not the mother (Hart 1955, 66).

This example illustrates that, even if the mother is harmed, the responsibility and potential apology are owed to the son. Being causally or agentially involved in causing harm to someone does not determine to whom an apology is owed, and thus the directionality of agential involvement does not explain the second-personal nature of apologies.

In summary, then, the example-based critique against the *Apology Principle* ultimately founders. It results not only in an intuitive impasse but also counterproductively necessitates the introduction of an alternative condition for an apology: agential or causal involvement. This condition fails to satisfy two crucial desiderata: it does not clearly differentiate between an apology and mere regret, nor does it convincingly explain the second-personal nature of apologies. Therefore, this approach to challenging the *Apology Principle* is unsuccessful.

Rejection of (3) The Driver's Apology

The paradigmatic example of an apology involves culpable conduct. Accordingly, several scholars have argued that fault, or culpability, is a requirement for a genuine apology, such that one cannot give a genuine apology for something unless one is also at fault for it (*cf* Bovens 2008, 221, 224; Scanlon 2008, 150; N Smith 2014, 20).

The solution of *Pascal's Apology* is a version of such a view. It also holds that fault is a requirement of a genuine apology, but it adds that absolute certainty of fault is not needed. If there is a high-stakes situation and at least the possibility of fault or culpability, this is enough for someone to give an apology.

So understood, *Pascal's Apology* needs to defend its implication that, under conditions of perfect knowledge, the driver ought not to apologise. If this is incorrect, then the reference to uncertainty about fault would be an erroneous workaround. Instead, something else, which may be perfectly clear in real-life cases, determines the need to apologise. Thus, I shall now focus on the driver's need to apologise under conditions of perfect knowledge.

Scanlon defends the view that *Pascal's Apology* implies. He states:

> Saying 'I'm sorry' is appropriate even in A's [eg the lorry driver's] case. But in his case this would not be an apology but an expression of regret at the tragic outcome of his action [because] [i]ts function would not be to admit a fault. (Scanlon 2008, 150)

However, several scholars disagreed with the idea that a genuine apology must involve admitting fault, or uncertainty about fault. They contend that even when someone causes harm through no fault of their own, they might still need to apologise. As Marc Cohen put it: an 'apology can be necessary (and effective) when the offender … is not morally blameworthy' (Cohen 2018, 593; see also BN Waller 2007, 452; Gardner 2018, 145; Capes 2019, 67; Piovarchy 2020, 149). And Paulina Sliwa even refers specifically to the lorry driver in her explication:

> [W]e apologise and expect apologies not just for grave intentional wrongdoing but also for wrongs that are excused, or justified, or minor. In such cases, apologies are apt but remorse may be uncalled for. Apologies are apt in cases of bad moral luck. Williams' lorry driver who hits a child can meaningfully apologise to its parents even when he is fully conscious of the fact that he was not at fault for the accident. (Sliwa 2023, 5)

In what follows, I shall outline what I deem to be the most persuasive argument in support of this view and claim that, suitably modified, it requires us to relinquish the view endorsed by Scanlon and implied by *Pascal's Apology*. The argument proceeds in three main steps.

The first step concerns faultless wrongdoing: scholars have argued that, even in cases of the faultless causing of harm, there is still a wrong, understood as an (excused) transgression of a moral norm. In the case of the lorry driver, this is the norm against hitting and killing people with a lorry. Sliwa provides an indication of this notion of wrongdoing:

> We commit wrongdoing – we act wrongly – when we perform some action that violates a norm, duty or infringes on a right. Wrongdoing, as I understand it, can be intentional or unintentional, justified or excused. (Sliwa 2023, 3; similar in Cohen 2018 and Capes 2019)

The second step concerns the change of the moral situation after the transgression of a moral norm. As Sliwa put it:

> Wrongdoing changes the normative landscape in a characteristic way. It creates reparative rights and duties – the duty to acknowledge the wrong done, to explain, to compensate – it changes the feeling and relationship rights and duties in play. (Sliwa 2023, 2)

There are different explanations as to what exactly happens. Some argue that, after committing a (faultless) wrong, *new* reasons or even obligations arise:

> [W]rongdoers often acquire *new* duties to try to repair the relationship with their victims, even if they are not deserving of blame for their wrongdoing.' (Piovarchy 2020, 148, emphasis changed)
>
> By engaging in wrongdoing, we place ourselves under *new* obligations and we give others new rights against us. (Sliwa 2023, 12, emphasis added)

Others think that it is still the old reasons or obligations whose normative force persists. John Gardner is the clearest proponent of this view. Gardner defends what he calls the 'continuity thesis':

> It is the thesis that the secondary obligation is a rational echo of the primary obligation, for it exists to serve, so far as may still be done, the reasons for the primary obligation that was not performed when its performance was due. (Gardner 2011, 33)

In cases of faultless harming, a person did not conform to an obligation, or reason. The continuity thesis claims that this person then ought to do the next best thing to minimise the departure from the original reason or obligation.

For our current discussion, it does not matter whether we agree with Piovarchy and Sliwa, who say *new* reasons for moral action arise, or with Gardner, who believes the *original* reasons still hold moral weight. What is important is understanding that when someone breaks a moral norm, even through no fault of his own, there is a moral expectation that this person react to the moral transgression in some way. It would not be morally acceptable just to ignore what occurred. Such indifference, especially in cases like that of the lorry driver, would be 'callous' (Cornford 2011, 45).

Finally, the third step of the argument claims that, in some cases of faultless wrongdoing, including the lorry driver's case, only an apology is the appropriate response to the transgression of a moral norm and the resulting change of the moral situation, and therefore apologies without fault ought to be recognised. Justin Capes comments about the lorry driver as follows: 'A failure to apologize would display a lack of concern … An apology is thus called for, despite the fact that you [ie the lorry driver] aren't blameworthy for what you did' (Capes 2019, 67).

Capes and others argue that apologising is crucial because it is the only way to prevent additional 'expressive harm'. Expressive harm occurs when someone fails to respond appropriately after doing something wrong. For example, if someone breaks a friend's valuable item and does not apologise and acknowledge their mistake, the friend might justifiably feel disrespected or uncared for. Equally, Capes and others argue, if the lorry driver does not apologise after running over the child, he might express disrespect to, and neglect for, the victim and their family.[5]

To substantiate the need for an apology, scholars often consider the contrast between two different responses of the lorry driver to the accident:

> If the driver apologizes profusely and tries to make up for his action, he is displaying a considerable level of positive regard toward the dead child and her parents. (Piovarchy 2020, 148)
>
> [I]f the driver denies any wrongdoing, treats the child's death as simply unlucky, and rejects having any new duties, he thereby displays a level of disregard for which we can blame him … (Piovarchy 2020, 148)

[5] Piovarchy provides a nuanced view of this sort. He says: 'Anyone who understood all the facts of Williams's lorry driver case could not reasonably interpret the driver as insulting or threatening the child.' (Piovarchy 2020, 155–156) Thus, there is no initial harm or insult. But Piovarchy adds that the way in which the driver reacts to what happened can very well carry expressive content. He says: 'there is a second way in which the social meaning account of wrongdoing can explain why the driver ought to make amends. This comes from the fact that one's actions after an excused wrongdoing *also* carry a social meaning' (Piovarchy 2020, 155–156). And avoiding such expressive harm requires an apology, Piovarchy argues.

> [I]f A [ie the lorry driver] does not apologize, then A's behavior (not apologizing, acting as if no harm was caused) does express the attitude that it is acceptable to mistreat or harm B. (Cohen 2018, 592).
>
> [An] apology counteracts the expressive harm caused by leaving the action unaddressed. (Cohen 2018, 593).[6]

These quotations make some persuasive points, most notably that offering an apology can convey respect and positive regard, whereas completely ignoring the accident can lead to offence and instantiate morally inacceptable behaviour. Yet, what the above scholars overlook, or at least fail to address explicitly, is a middle ground that exists between these two extremes. This third option, which also Scanlon highlights, involves expressing regret and showing empathy without necessarily delivering a genuine apology. This is a nuanced approach whereby the person acknowledges the incident and its impact, demonstrates understanding and concern, and yet stops short of a full apology. By expressing regret and empathy, one can still address the harm caused and show care for those affected, without giving a full apology or showing total disregard.[7]

To overcome this weakness in the argument, we require further support for the conclusion that an apology, rather than mere expression of regret, is apt in the case of the lorry driver. And it is here that I aim to go beyond other scholars' accounts and bolster the third step of the argument in favour of apologies without fault. I suggest that two aspects, namely relations and timing, to support the view that the driver ought to apologise, rather than merely express regret.

Earlier, I highlighted the relational nature of an apology to support the *Apology Principle*, ie the claim that a necessary condition of an (appropriate) apology is responsibility, rather than mere agential involvement. I shall now highlight the relational nature of apologies again, but this time to support another view, namely that the driver ought to apologise, rather than merely express regret. The argument proceeds from a description of the kind of response we morally expect from the driver to the conclusion that an apology instantiates this kind of response better than the expression of regret.

I take it that we morally expect the driver to address the parents of the victim, and not just anyone. In other words, what we expect from the driver is a genuinely second-personal, or interpersonal, component – namely that he

[6] Capes brought in an aspect of uncertainty or suspicion which I left aside: 'when we injure others in a way that evinces, or could reasonably be suspected to evince, ill will or lack of due regard, we have an obligation to apologize for the injury even if we aren't to blame for it. This obligation, it seems, is grounded in the value of repairing and maintaining relationships that are damaged or threatened by our injurious behavior. Apologizing in such cases is essential to protecting the relationship from further harm (for example, by reassuring the victim of the injurer's good will going forward), and will, in many cases at least, go some way to repairing whatever damage to the relationship may already have been done.' (Capes 2019, 67).

[7] This view might be close to those of Bovens (2008) and Scanlon (2008, 150).

did, in fact, address those he harmed, including his victim's family. Those who argue that the driver ought to express regret cannot automatically account for this relational dimension since the expression of regret, as an emotion, does not already have a designated addressee. By contrast, an apology has a relational element built into its very idea, as it is always about apologising *to someone*. In fact, an apology would be unintelligible without an addressee. Thus, when we attend to the second-personal dimension of the required response from the driver, we can see that an apology immediately accounts for it, while an expression of regret does not. In this respect, the view favouring an apology has an explanatory advantage and captures more morally relevant details of the lorry driver's situation.

In addition to this explanatory advantage, there is also a moral dimension linked to this relational aspect that makes an apology more fitting than an expression of regret. Commenting on the lorry driver's case, Sussman said:

> [T]he immediate aftermath of the accident is just not the time to offer excuses, plead for one-self, or turn attention away from the primary calamity (the death of a child) and onto the much less important question of what this properly means for the driver. (Sussman 2018, 801)

Sussman is right that the driver ought not to focus on what the accident properly means *for him*. He ought not to make *his* defence and lack of culpability the centre of attention. Doing so would be inappropriately self-centred. Rather, the driver ought to attend to *the parents' loss* and explicitly *address them* as the parents of the child and as harmed parties themselves. But if so, it also seems that the expression of regret is less appropriate than an apology. (Agent)-regret is, at root, a feeling and its expression is therefore principally the driver's report on his own inner life – the sorrow he feels as a result of killing the child. By contrast, apologies are not, like regret, inward-looking, but rather outward-looking. When apologising, the primary focus is on the moral significance of other people's loss, rather than on one's own feelings. Thus, insofar as what is morally required of the driver is not a self-centred report on how *he feels* about his involvement in the accident but rather a focus on the *moral significance of other people's loss* caused by that accident, the driver ought to apologise rather than merely express regret.

The second important aspect of the driver's response, which – in addition to the relational aspect – aligns more closely with an apology than the expression of regret, concerns the *timing* of the expected response from the driver. I suggest the driver choose an appropriate time to approach the parents, ensuring they are ready to engage with him. Approaching them too early and focusing the interaction on them, as well as waiting too long and creating the impression of indifference, could both be morally problematic. Given this assumption, we can ask which concept – regret or apology – would be the better practical guide when the lorry driver thinks about what to do. In other words, when deciding how to act, is it more helpful for the driver to think in terms of expressing regret or of offering an apology?

As far as apologies are concerned, timing is a key aspect. As Shuman, Jeffrey Helmreich and others have explicitly emphasised, a proper apology must be delivered at the right time. Sometimes, delaying an apology can be morally wrong, and at other times, forcing an apology too soon, before someone is ready to receive it, can be equally morally wrong (Helmreich 2015, 82–83; Shuman 2000, 186). Thus, when the driver intends to apologise, he will have to consider aspects of timing as they are also key to his interaction with others after the accident.

By contrast, the expression of regret seems to be the less appropriate response. If the driver aims to express solely regret, he has reason to choose a moment that allows for a genuine expression of this emotion, ie when *his* feelings are most sincere and can be communicated authentically. In other words, the driver's concern will be choosing the best time to express his emotions. However, this is mistaken. The driver's focus should be on what the parents are due and ready to accept. Therefore, prioritising the expression of regret seems to conflict with both the timing aspect and the primary considerations involved.

Admittedly, one may impose constraints on when the driver ought to express his regret and say that he only ought to do so when the time is right. But there are two problems with this response. First, it may be that his feeling of regret has by then vanished, thereby no longer allowing him to express it authentically. Second, this response inaccurately describes the considerations about the parents as *constraints* on expressing emotions, rather than as the *guiding reasons* in the first place. On this view, it may seem that the driver first thinks about how to express his regret properly and then considers how this aligns with the parents' perspectives, whereas the correct view would start with the parents' perspectives.

Thus, the timing requirement of the driver's response is integral to apologies, but an external addition to the expression of regret. Therefore, in this respect too, the view favouring an apology has an explanatory advantage and captures the morally relevant details of the lorry driver's situation more appropriately.

This brings my argument to a conclusion: apologies without fault can be defended and, therefore, *Pascal's Apology* (which still clings on to a requirement of fault) is an unconvincing workaround. The driver's need to apologise does not depend on fault, or the possibility of fault under uncertainty, but instead on the fact that he transgressed a norm and caused harm to others. Thus, the *Lorry Driver Paradox* still stands.

This conclusion is also significant for Part I as a whole, as it supports the version of the *Apology Principle* that establishes responsibility as a necessary condition for apology – without requiring it to be framed in terms of fault or culpability, but instead grounding it in answerability. Moreover, the arguments in this chapter further clarify why and when someone who is answerable for harm ought to apologise (eg to avoid further 'expressive harm'), while acknowledging that answerability by itself does not necessarily entail an obligation to apologise.

Let me now consider a couple of objections.

OBJECTIONS

Objection 1: Victimhood of Driver and Co-responsibility of Others

This objection argues against the notion that the driver should apologise, focusing on two key considerations: the driver's own victimhood and the co-responsibility of others. Concerning the former, the driver is not only an agent involved in the accident but also a victim of it. The driver's victimhood encompasses various aspects, such as being inadvertently involved in a tragic event, facing unexpected and traumatic circumstances, and potentially dealing with the psychological aftermath. These factors contribute to a complex emotional and mental state for the driver, who may be grappling with shock, trauma and guilt. Expecting the driver to apologise in such a state could be seen as overlooking his experience of victimhood and the accompanying psychological distress.

Moving to the co-responsibility of other parties, other important aspects arise. The accident's occurrence was not solely due to the driver's actions; other entities played crucial roles. For instance, the lorry company could have contributed to the accident, such as through vehicle-maintenance or its operational policies. The parents, too, may have contributed through aspects of their conduct or decisions that indirectly influenced the events leading to the accident. These factors suggest a shared causality where multiple parties collectively contributed to the incident's occurrence. Thus, the objection argues that placing the entire responsibility for an apology on the driver disregards these crucial aspects.

In response to the objection, it is important to note that the involvement of others in the situation does not necessarily preclude the driver's need to apologise. This perspective is supported by Luc Bovens, who suggests that there are scenarios where mutual apologies are appropriate. As Bovens puts it: 'Should parties to a row apologize for blowing up at each other? Should spouses apologize to each other when both have had extra-marital affairs?' (Bovens 2008, 232). This concept of mutual apologies implies that multiple parties can bear responsibility and offer apologies simultaneously.

Hence, while we should indeed consider the responses of other parties involved, it does not undermine the conclusion that the lorry driver may also need to apologise. To call the driver responsible does not imply that he is *solely* responsible or that others might not also have an obligation to apologise. The driver's responsibility and subsequent apology can coexist with the responsibilities of other parties involved in the incident. Moreover, the way in which the driver can be required to apologise could be sensitive to the driver's own experience and the psychological harm he suffered because of the accident.

Therefore, a more robust version of the objection would need to demonstrate that the shared responsibility of other parties diminishes or alters the driver's own responsibility towards them, including the appropriateness of offering an apology. In absence of such evidence, the driver's apology remains a valid and potentially necessary response, alongside the consideration of apologies from other responsible parties.

Objection 2: Inappropriate Acceptance of Apology

The second objection posits that the driver's apology, if it cannot be fittingly accepted, should not be considered genuine. This argument hinges on the premise that a genuine apology is contingent on the appropriateness of being accepted by its recipient(s). If the moral expectation is for the recipients to refuse the apology, deeming it unnecessary, it could indicate that an apology is either misplaced or superficial.

In considering this, it is worth questioning whether the appropriateness of accepting an apology completely dictates the appropriateness of offering one. It seems entirely possible that there is a moral obligation for someone to apologise, while for the recipients, it might be commendable either to contextualise it in a way that acknowledges no inherent fault in the action being apologised for, or even to refuse to accept it.

Moreover, in the context of the lorry driver case, the appropriate response from the parents is a matter of debate in the first place, and I believe that they could appropriately accept the driver's apology. The parents could receive it with gratitude, recognising it as a symbol of shared values and an effort to overcome the tragedy. The apology could signify to the parents the driver's acknowledgment of the gravity of the event so that they may relieve him of further moral obligations towards them. Given the severity of the incident, a response of 'no apology needed' seems inappropriate.

In essence, this scenario opens up a broader discussion about the dynamics of apologising and receiving apologies, especially in complex and emotionally charged situations like that of the lorry driver and the parents. But, as it stands, the objection does not challenge the view that the driver ought to apologise.

Objection 3: Defence Precludes Apology

Charles Griswold argues that '[an] apology and the request for forgiveness assume … that an *excuse* is not being offered' (Griswold 2007, 143, original emphasis). Govier and Verwoerd add that an 'apology … will be weakened if it includes attempted justifications or excuses' (Govier and Verwoerd 2002, 67). This perspective has two sides: first, *if* people apologise, then they should not also offer a defence like an excuse or justification, as this would somehow undermine the sincerity of their apology; second, there is the following contraposition of the previous conditional: *if* people do have a defence such as an excuse or justification, then they no longer need to apologise. In short: defence precludes apology. But if this is true, the lorry driver ought not to apologise, because (as we have assumed), he has a full excuse.

This challenge is insightful but partially misguides by implying all defences eliminate the need for an apology, when in fact only some defences do. By way of elaboration: if people have adequate grounds for either being *exempt from* responsibility (eg by lacking capacity or competence) or for *denying* their involvement in the alleged act, then they have a 'defence' that negates the need for an apology. This is because, in these cases, the individual is not just free from liability to blame or punishment, but also from the obligation to answer for their actions, ie from responsibility as answerability. And, per the *Apology Principle*, without such responsibility, the need for an apology cannot arise.

However, the scenario is different with excuses and justifications. While exemptions and denials negate responsibility altogether, excuses and justifications acknowledge the responsibility to answer for actions, only disputing the liability to blame or punishment. Therefore, a complete excuse (for instance, due to non-culpable ignorance or faultless accidents) may eliminate fault or liability but not necessarily negate the responsibility to answer for one's actions, hence still allowing for an apology.[8]

Justifications, though, are more intricate. While excuses acknowledge the occurrence of wrongdoing or a transgression of norms, justifications challenge the very existence of wrongdoing from the outset. This distinction is crucial when considering apologies, which I believe inherently imply some form of wrongdoing or transgression of norms. To deal with this complexity, we need to distinguish between two kinds of justifications.

Some justifications, like those for proportionate self-defence, completely deny any form of wrongdoing or transgression of norms. In these scenarios, there is no basis for an apology because no wrong is recognised. However, other justifications, particularly those involving choosing a lesser evil, present a different case. Take, for example, Thomas Nagel's scenario where twisting someone's arm could be justified to prevent greater harm (Nagel 1986, 176). In this situation, although the act of arm-twisting may be justified overall, it still constitutes a wronging of the individual and a breach of a moral norm. Therefore, in such circumstances, offering an apology to the individual who was wronged, despite the broader justification, remains valid and appropriate.

[8] Note, however, that this position relies on the view defended earlier, namely that apologies do not require fault or moral culpability.

Thus, the relationship between defences and apologies can be outlined as follows: a sincere apology, per the *Apology Principle*, requires the apologising party to be responsible and to have transgressed a norm. Some defences, like exemptions and denials, remove responsibility, while others, such as some justifications, show that no norm was transgressed. In these instances, an apology is not suitable. However, other defences, like excuses, cases of wronging without overall wrongdoing, and lesser evil scenarios, acknowledge both responsibility and the transgression of norms, making them compatible with a genuine apology.

Objection 4: The Driver cannot Satisfy the Conditions of a Genuine Apology

The driver's apology represents a departure from the typical cognitive and conative conditions of an apology. A paradigmatic apology is coupled with the cognitive (or doxastic) requirement that one have a 'specific belief about the morally relevant features of the situation that made one's performance transgressive [of moral norms]' (Davis 2002, 170). But the Pascalian driver does not have a firm belief such as this. He only leaves open the possibility of his having transgressed a moral norm as one option among others.

Moreover, paradigmatic apologies are coupled with the conative requirement that the offending party is expected to show 'a willingness to change its ways' (Bovens 2008, 220). But for the lorry driver, it may not be clear what he should change, or indeed whether he should change anything at all, in the future. In fact, Sussman explicitly denies that this is what the lorry driver does or should do:

> Unlike a normal apology, the driver's quasi-apology does not need to express any sort of general, forward-looking resolution, but only one that is inherently singular and retrospective, something along the lines of 'would that I could undo this particular thing I have done'. (Sussman 2018, 806)

Therefore, one may argue, the driver's apology fails to be genuine.

In response, it should be noted that the deviation from these typical conditions is a direct response to the uncertainty in the driver's situation; it reflects the driver's proper understanding of the circumstances, and it does not make the driver's apology any less sincere or more problematic. The driver seriously considers the possibility of having violated certain norms, and remains open to altering his behaviour if new information suggests he should. For this reason, the driver avoids the pitfalls normally associated with not meeting these typical cognitive and conative conditions. And given the approximation of the conditions to the greatest extent possible, the driver's apology remains apt. (On approaching the conditions of paradigmatic apologies, see also Miller (2014).)

CONCLUSION

In this chapter, I have discussed a solution to the *Lorry Driver Paradox* that is anchored in the idea that real-life accident scenarios are inherently uncertain. By incorporating modal qualifiers and insights from *Pascal's Wager*, I presented an approach to apologies, called *Pascal's Apology,* which could reconcile the apparent inconsistency in the *Lorry Driver Paradox* and explicate the reasons for apologising. Moreover, this approach might be especially appealing to those who believe that fault is essential for a sincere apology. However, by challenging this belief, I have rejected *Pascal's Apology* as a convincing solution, and I have thereby given more weight to the *Lorry Driver Paradox*. While *Pascal's Apology* offers a useful perspective in real-life situations, it falls short as a comprehensive solution to the paradox's inherent contradiction.

5

The Strictness First Approach

I HAVE SO far developed two feasible solutions to the *Lorry Driver Paradox*, one based on the idea of strict moral answerability, and another based on the normative power of taking responsibility; and I have rejected the solution based on *Pascal's Apology*. But with two solutions at hand, the question arises as to which of them ought to be preferred, or even whether they could be combined.

There are two reasons to prefer strict moral answerability over taking responsibility. First, strict moral answerability offers the same explanatory value as taking responsibility, viz it also explains how to avoid the inconsistency in the *Lorry Driver Paradox*, but it is simpler than the normative power of taking responsibility. It was necessary for the latter to postulate the existence of a normative power of taking responsibility, spell out the conditions for the exercise of such a power, and distinguish between different senses of 'ought'. By contrast, strict moral answerability only introduces a distinction between answerability and liability, and the simple idea that moral answerability is *strict*.

Second, the idea of taking responsibility is parasitic on – ie cannot be conceived without – the idea of strict moral answerability. As I outlined in my discussion of taking responsibility, the type of responsibility, or answerability, that can be taken is markedly different from the type of responsibility, or answerability, that philosophers normally describe. This is because this type of responsibility will not rely on fault or the reflection of someone's quality of judgment. The only type of responsibility that can be taken at will is strict answerability. For this reason, strict moral answerability is more fundamental than the idea of taking responsibility as a normative power. Hence, strict moral answerability must be part of the overall solution in any case.

However, there are also considerations that support the normative power of taking responsibility. To begin with, I defended a restricted scope of strict moral answerability, ie a scope that is narrower than in Duff's initial proposal and that excludes cases like Thomson's *Day's End*. In these cases, strict moral answerability no longer applies. The normative power of taking responsibility could come into play here and provide agents with an opportunity to extend their responsibility. In these cases in particular, the value of the normative power of taking responsibility, as described in chapter three, could be significant.

Moreover, strict moral answerability may sometimes also depend on the idea of taking responsibility, and not just the other way around. Strict moral answerability had a two-part sufficient condition: people are answerable whenever (a) they cause (or causally contribute to) a type of harm which (b) they had an obligation to guard against. In contexts where multiple people causally contribute to, or cause, specific types of harm, it may be the case that many people will become answerable, maybe even so many that it becomes unfeasible to hold all of them answerable at once. In such cases, individuals could 'take responsibility' and identify themselves as bearers of responsibility amidst a great number of people, and thereby facilitate practices of holding each other answerable. Without such a voluntary and non-arbitrary way of taking responsibility, strict moral answerability might create problems in practice. I shall explain these situations in greater detail in Part II, as I think they arise prominently in the context of AI.

Overall, then, we can see that the normative power of taking responsibility also has some advantages, but that they gain real traction only if we go beyond the confines of the *Lorry Driver Paradox* and consider cases in which strict moral answerability either no longer applies (eg in Thomson's *Day's End*) or creates an impractical abundance of responsibility (which I shall discuss in Part II). For this reason, I suggest the *strictness first approach*, which considers strict moral answerability to be the correct solution to the *Lorry Driver Paradox*, thereby acknowledging strict moral answerability as the most fundamental concept, but also affords a secondary role to the normative power of taking responsibility, thereby acknowledging the potentially significant part this idea could play in other cases. In Part II, I shall return to these ideas and elaborate them in the context of artificial intelligence (AI).

However, before proceeding, I wish to state one further result from Part I, namely the hypothesis of a *Legal Lead* in the context of responsibility. The *Legal Lead* is the methodological claim that we can advance our understanding of moral responsibility by investigating legal responsibility. Philosophers usually assume that it is the other way around, ie that the accounts of moral responsibility guide how we ought to understand and construct legal responsibility. But in Part I, I highlighted two areas where an investigation into legal responsibility can promote an investigation into moral responsibility. In chapter two I showed how the criminal law on reverse burdens of proof has developed a form of strict answerability, which is currently missing in our philosophical frameworks on moral responsibility. In chapter three I argued that the international public law on waiving state immunity informs an account of the normative power of taking responsibility by declaration, which is also currently missing in our philosophical frameworks on moral responsibility. Both approaches were highly significant in the context of the *Lorry Driver Paradox*. Thus, my discussion also provided new evidence on how legal scholarship can help us understand moral responsibility. This claim will be supported further when I demonstrate that the ideas of Part I also help us deal with the challenges surrounding AI in Part II.

Part II

Artificial Intelligence

6

The Autonomous AI Conundrum

ARTIFICIAL INTELLIGENCE (AI) is increasingly taking on tasks once thought to be exclusively within human domains: from digital assistants engaging in conversations, to self-driving cars (Dubber, Pasquale and Das 2020), to complex medical procedures (Shademan et al 2016; Ficuciello et al 2019; Schiff and Borenstein 2019), and even recruitment processes. But not only is AI handling tasks in these domains, it can sometimes also outperform humans, as it is already the case in some domains of medical diagnostics. The potential benefits are immense and relevant areas include not only healthcare but also autonomous driving and other fields where processing a large volume of information or rapid response times are key to success (Kiener 2021, 2022).

Unfortunately, the best AI also tends to be the least controllable and the least transparent. It is the least controllable because, among other reasons, some of its processes are too fast to be monitored in real time; and it is the least transparent because some of its technological bases, eg deep neural networks, create 'black boxes' with impenetrably complex algorithms. However, the ability to control and anticipate outcomes is key to human moral responsibility. So, how could anyone ever be morally responsible when such sophisticated yet uncontrollable and opaque AI causes harm, eg when an autonomous car runs over a pedestrian, when a surgical robot paralyses a patient, or when an autonomous weapon system kills a non-combatant?

This question triggered a controversial debate over whether AI creates 'responsibility gaps', ie situations in which no one is morally responsible for the harm caused by AI.[1] Some scholars have argued that the use of AI creates responsibility gaps (Sparrow 2007; Danaher 2016; Gunkel 2017; Matthias 2004; De Jong 2020) precisely because it removes control and understanding, whereas others have denied the existence of such gaps (Schulzke 2013; Johnson 2015; Himmelreich 2019; Tigard 2020). Still others have endorsed an intermediate position, arguing that gaps exist but that they are narrower than usually imagined (Simpson and Müller 2016; Nyholm 2020, ch 3).[2]

[1] For other formulations of what a 'responsibility gap' is, see Himmelreich (2019) and List (2021).
[2] This introduction is based on the introduction in Kiener (2022).

In the first half of this book, I introduced and addressed the *Lorry Driver Paradox*, a paradox about how we think about moral responsibility in general. In this second part of the book, I shall turn my focus to responsibility in the context of AI, and, more particularly, to the challenge that I think parallels the *Lorry Driver Paradox* and which I shall call the *Autonomous AI Conundrum*. The *Autonomous AI Conundrum* concerns cases in which generally beneficent, yet also uncontrollable and opaque AI systems, cause harm, eg when an autonomous vehicle runs over a pedestrian, or a surgical robot paralyses a patient. I shall argue that, since the *Autonomous AI Conundrum* resembles the *Lorry Driver Paradox* in its key features, we can connect specialist AI ethics with traditional moral philosophy in new ways. More specifically, my main aim will be to import my results about strict moral answerability and taking responsibility as a normative power to the debate on AI ethics and thereby break new ground in this debate. But before I do so, let me first describe in greater detail the responsibility challenge in the context of AI.

THE *AUTONOMOUS AI CONUNDRUM*

It is 7 May 2016 near Williston, Florida. A black Tesla glides silently along the highway, but suddenly the traffic comes to a standstill. A blinding ray of sunlight hits the car's windshield, and its brakes are applied too late. A collision occurs and one person dies. Who is responsible for this tragedy? The person sitting in the driving seat? But none of the passengers were driving. It was an AI that controlled the car.[3]

This case resembles Williams's original lorry driver case. In both scenarios, people act in ways that cause serious harm to others, ie by steering the lorry in Williams's case or by making the autonomous car take a certain route in the Tesla case. Moreover, in both cases (let us assume), the people causing the harm are not at fault because they could not possibly have foreseen the accident, were unable to prevent it when it happened, and did not display any other flaw in their conduct. Yet, as with Williams's original lorry driver, those involved in the use, and potentially also the development of the Tesla are likely feel appropriate 'agent-regret' (Williams 1981, 27), ie the wish, accompanied by sadness, that the circumstances connected to their agency had been different. In fact, in both scenarios, it would seem morally appalling if these people did not feel any agent-regret, but simply shrugged off the accident. We might also expect the passengers, the owner of the car, or those involved in the development of the autonomous car, to apologise for what happened.

[3] This is a slightly modified version of a real event.

On this basis, we may formulate what I call the *Autonomous AI Conundrum*, which parallels the *Lorry Driver Paradox* and consists of the following individually plausible but jointly inconsistent claims:

1* The users and developers of the AI-powered car are not morally responsible for the person's death.
2* *Apology Principle*: one ought to apologise only if one is morally responsible for certain harm.
3* Someone among the users or developers of the AI-powered car ought to apologise.

Let us take a closer look at this inconsistent triad.[4]

Claim 1: No Responsibility

Once the lorry is no longer operated by the human driver but instead by an AI system, concerns about the lack of moral responsibility increase. Even more clearly than before, it seems that the passengers are not genuinely morally responsible. Starting with control: in the case of autonomous vehicles, the passengers of the car have even less control over the vehicle's actions than a human driver of a non-autonomous vehicle does. While a human driver of a non-autonomous vehicle can still make decisions while the vehicle is in operation, the user or owner of an autonomous vehicle is largely reliant on the vehicle's programming and sensors. Therefore, if a human driver of a non-autonomous vehicle, like Williams's lorry driver, is not responsible due to limited control, the user of an autonomous vehicle is even less so. But it is not just the user or owner of the car, but also the developers, who lack control. Consider the following three aspects.

First, there is the inability to intervene: AI systems may operate too fast or be used in too remote an area for humans to intervene. Robert Sparrow explained how this is true in cases of military applications (Sparrow 2007), but I maintain that this is also true of conventional vehicles. Neither the owner nor the developers of the car had any meaningful opportunity to intervene in the situation at hand.

Second, there is the 'autonomy' of AI systems: AI systems make independent decisions, and thereby disconnect from the agency, control and decision-making of humans, whether the users or the developers of the AI. To say that AI systems are 'autonomous' means something other than saying that they are 'automatic', ie a distinction that is often overlooked[5] but already present in Ancient

[4] Although I focused on the case of an autonomous car, the scope of my discussion will include other similar autonomous AI systems too, eg in the context of healthcare or the military.

[5] An exception is the US Department of Defence, 2011, 43.

Greek. Drawing on Homer, I assume that something is auto-matic when it is fully pre-programmed and performs tasks without immediate control by other agents. For instance, Homer describes how doors of the Olympus open 'automatically' when someone approaches them.[6] Drawing on Aristotle, I assume that something is auto-'nomous' when, in addition to its ability to execute tasks without immediate control by other agents, it also sets its own rules. In Aristotle's political philosophy, cities are autonomous insofar as they determine their own laws and are not dependent on another political entity regarding the rules that govern them (Aristotle 1959 (Politics)). I argue that the distinction between 'automatic' and 'autonomous' informs the technological reality of deep neural networks since these technologies are not just 'automatic', ie they are not fully pre-programmed by humans, like an espresso machine. Rather, they are 'autonomous' insofar as they learn from their environment and shape the very rules and principles according to which they operate. And this dimension of autonomy means that they are further disconnected from human agency, and thus afford us less control over them.

Third, there is the 'problem of many hands' (Poel, Royakkers and Zwart 2015): there are many people involved in the development and use of AI. However, none of them has more than a tiny proportion of control over AI's outcomes, such that a great disparity arises between the severity of the outcome and the actual contribution, making the attribution of responsibility increasingly difficult or even impossible. Thus, not only the users of AI but also the developers of AI have a significant lack of control.

Moving on to the epistemic condition and foreseeability, a similar picture arises. The users and developers of an autonomous vehicle have even less foresight into potential accidents than a human driver of a non-autonomous vehicle. The human driver can anticipate and react to situations based on experience and judgment, whereas users and developers of an autonomous vehicle again largely depend on the vehicle's 'autonomous' algorithms. Thus, if a lack of foresight precludes the lorry driver's responsibility, it does so even more in the case of the user and developers of an autonomous vehicle.

We can also use further considerations to support this point. To begin with, AI systems behind autonomous vehicles, eg deep neural networks, make it very difficult to understand how they work, even for experts. This is because of the sheer complexity of these systems, which base a single output, eg a diagnosis, on about 23 million parameters, and also because AI systems are able to learn from data without human supervision, while constantly changing their own algorithm (Kiener 2021). In addition, what we are faced with is never just one single technology or AI system, but an assemblage of different interacting technologies, and this creates a problem of 'many things', where it can be virtually

[6] See Homer: Odyssey: Book 5, 749; Book 18, 376.

impossible to identify the causal structures behind something like an accident, or to foresee which feature might play an important role in future critical situations. Moreover, AI systems constantly change their own algorithms, leaving little time to scrutinise the status quo. So, even if one understands how an AI system works at one point, the situation may be altogether different at a later point. Thus, both users and developers face serious obstacles in understanding the best-performing AI systems and may, therefore, fail to satisfy the epistemic condition of responsibility.

Finally, a similar result arises from the perspective of those who advocate a quality-of-will approach to responsibility. In the original paradox, the driver's quality of will (intentions, moral character) is not questioned because the accident happens despite their best efforts to avoid it. In the case of an autonomous vehicle, the user's quality of will is even further removed from the incident. The vehicle's actions reflect the programming and design, not the user's moral character or intentions. Therefore, if the driver's quality of will is not implicated in the accident, the user's is even less so. Furthermore, the developer's quality of will may not be reflected in the accident either, given the systems' ability to learn and adjust their performance in an 'autonomous' way, as explained above, and thus disconnect from the thoughts, choices and intentions of those who developed the AI.

These considerations make a strong *a fortiori* argument: if we do not consider the lorry driver genuinely morally responsible, we have even less justification to consider the people involved in developing and using autonomous AI systems as responsible when things go wrong. Yet, as before, this is only a preliminary argument against responsibility, and one which we will have to reconsider in Part II of this book.

Claim 2: Apology Principle

In Part I, I argued for the view that one ought to apologise for something only if one is morally responsible for it, and two solutions suggested that responsibility could be understood as strict moral answerability. Since this is meant to be a general principle which applies across different contexts, I shall rely here on my previous arguments.

Claim 3: Someone Ought to Apologise

As in the lorry driver case, it seems that the users or developers of the autonomous car also have three types of reasons to apologise. First, there are aretaic reasons: given their involvement in the accident, it can be virtuous for them to apologise. In so doing, they could 'ease the pain or provide comfort to the grieving family' (Wolf 2001, 14), 'lessen the psychological burden [for the family]' (MacKenzie 2017, 110), and help the family to 'heal emotionally'. Thus, by apologising, these people would also act virtuously: they would accept a potential burden to themselves to benefit others and thereby refuse to be a person who is 'more concerned with saving face than helping others' (MacKenzie 2017, 110).

Second, there are deontic reasons: it is not only virtuous to apologise, but also obligatory. We may think that Adam Smith's description of a lorry driver-type case applies here too: 'To make no apology, to offer no atonement, is regarded as the highest brutality' (Adam Smith 2009, 125, Part II, Section III, Chapter II). Brutality implies that not apologising would be an offence to those who have been harmed as well as to their relatives. Thus, the passengers of the car may need to apologise so as not to 'gratuitously insult, offend, or humiliate others' (Kim 2014, 211).

Third, there are reasons linked to our status as a person. As mentioned in Part I, Wolf claimed that there is value in 'expressing our recognition that we are beings who are thoroughly in-the-world, in interaction with others whose movements and thoughts we cannot fully control, and whom we affect and are affected by accidentally as well as intentionally, involuntarily, unwittingly, inescapably, as well as voluntarily and deliberately' (Wolf 2001, 14). Wolf suggests that expressing this recognition and acknowledging our place as agents in the world requires not only accepting that harm stemmed from one's action, but also apologising for it. Failing to do so conflicts with a proper understanding of ourselves as persons who are 'in-the-world' and also 'defines an approach to life that is unhealthy and undesirable' (Wolf 2001, 13). Arguably, this applies not only to the lorry driver but also to people who direct and develop an autonomous vehicle in a way that includes an accident.

So, how should we deal with this inconsistent triad? Can we use the solutions and results developed in the general context of moral responsibility from Part I and apply them to the more specific setting of artificial intelligence?

7

*The Abundance of Strict Moral Answerability**

AMAZON'S ALEXA TELLS a ten-year-old girl to touch a live plug with a penny, encouraging her to do what could lead to severe burns or even the loss of an entire limb.[1] A self-driving Tesla tests its fully autonomous mode but it fails to recognise an upcoming bend and crashes, killing two people[2] (Kiener 2021; Bathaee 2018). Many scholars worry that, in such cases, the use of AI causes so called *responsibility gaps*, i.e. situations in which no one is morally responsible for the harm caused by AI, because no one seems to have the required control or foresight to be morally responsible for the harmful outcomes of such AI systems (Sparrow 2007; Coeckelbergh 2020; Nyholm 2020). In this chapter, I acknowledge that there is a significant challenge around responsibility and AI. Yet, I don't think that this challenge is best captured in terms of a responsibility *gap*. Instead, I argue for the opposite view, namely that there is responsibility *abundance*, i.e. a situation in which *numerous* agents are responsible for the harm caused by AI, and that the challenge comes from the difficulties in dealing with such abundance in practice. I shall support proceed in four steps. I first outline the type of moral responsibility I am interested in, namely 'strict moral answerability' and then, second, present a further argument for its existence. I then, third, show how strict moral answerability leads to an abundance (rather than gap) of responsibility in the context of AI and, fourth, use this result to reframe the challenge around responsibility and AI in terms a novel dilemma. I conclude by arguing that reframing the challenge in this way offers distinct dialectic and theoretical advantages, promising to help overcome some obstacles in the current debate surrounding 'responsibility gaps'.

Applied to the *Autonomous AI Conundrum*, focusing on autonomous driving, this approach would parallel the solution from chapter two in Part I, and it could be presented as follows:

1a* The users and developers of the AI-powered car ***are not*** **morally liable, ie blameworthy** for the person's death.

* Significant parts of this chapter appeared first in Kiener (2025).

[1] www.bbc.com/news/technology-59810383.

[2] www.theguardian.com/technology/2021/apr/19/two-die-in-tesla-crash-no-one-in-drivers-seat-police.

1b* The users and developers of the AI-powered car ***are*** **(strictly) morally answerable** for the person's death.

2** *Apology Principle*: one ought to apologise only if one is morally **answerable** for a certain harm.

3** Someone among the users or developers of the AI-powered car, **or even all of them**, ought to apologise.

THE CONCEPT OF STRICT MORAL ANSWERABILITY

I continue to understand responsibility in terms of moral answerability, as opposed to responsibility in terms of liability or blameworthiness. More specifically, I will continue to endorse the previously outlined definition and condition of strict moral answerability. As a *definition* of moral answerability, I endorse the view that 'a morally responsible [ie answerable] agent is one who can intelligibly be asked to "answer for" her attitudes and conduct' (Angela Smith 2015, 103), where 'to answer for' means 'to give her (justificatory) reasons for thinking, feeling, or acting in the way she has' (Angela Smith 2015, 103) (Scanlon 2000, ch 6). Thus, morally answering is not about giving purely causal explanations of one's conduct (eg by pointing to the psychological or neurological causes of one's action). Rather, it is about explaining one's motivation and the good one saw in one's conduct. For this reason, a morally answerable person plays a very different role compared to an eyewitness, who merely provides a detached report on what happened. Furthermore, there are times when not only it is reasonable to expect an answer from the responsible party, but also they are obliged to provide one when asked, particularly when asked by those they have harmed and who have the right to seek such an answer (Duff 2009a, ch 1).[3]

Alongside this *definition* of moral answerability, I propose the following sufficient *condition* (which I also first introduced in chapter two): a person is morally answerable for some harm if that person caused the harm and had a prospective obligation to guard against such harm. Thus, there are two constituents: a causation-clause and an obligation-clause. This means that answerability arises when a person causes harm during an activity, where the nature of the activity obliges them to guard against said harm. But it does *not* mean that answerability is restricted to those situations where guarding against some harm alone would already preclude the harm, ie guarantee that the harm will not occur.

[3] So understood, moral answerability often serves an investigative role: we demand answers to find out whether people lived up to their obligations. However, moral answerability can also persist when there is no uncertainty about a person's due diligence. Consider the lorry driver case, outlined below. Even if the child's family already knew exactly what happened and (let us assume) knew that the driver took due care, they still retain an entitlement and possibly an emotional need, to hear that very fact *from the driver*, and the driver still owes them an answer in this regard. The family's knowledge does not undermine the driver's obligation to comply with their requests for justification and explanation, and thus does not undermine the driver's answerability. (See Kiener 2024.).

Conversely, answerability is not restricted to situations where the existence of harm would imply that there must have been some form of infringement, violation or other insufficient regard for the prospective obligation. It is a key feature of my proposed view that answerability can arise and persist even if a person fully satisfies her obligations, but still causes harm due to bad luck.

My proposed *definition* of moral answerability is widely accepted, whereas its *condition* will again spark controversy and constitute the novelty of my proposed view. It is this condition that forms my proposed account into a view about *strict* moral answerability, where 'strict' means, roughly, that there is no requirement of fault, negligence or ill will on the part of the answerable person. The condition is met whenever a person causes a particular type of harm, which she had an obligation to guard against.

So far, I have simply re-stated my previous view, already illustrated by Williams's lorry driver, who is, in my view, strictly morally answerable. To say that the driver is answerable means that, following my definition, not only is it reasonable and appropriate to ask him to answer for his role in the accident, but also certain others also have the standing or right to demand an answer. The driver is then obliged to explain why he acted as he did, assure others he acted with due care, and acknowledge his responsibility to certain others – in his case the victim and their family. When things are clear, eg when it is known that the driver was not at fault, the 'answer' or 'explanation' expected can be short but sufficient. Something like 'I did my best, but I failed, and that failure was beyond my control' does not only provide the necessary facts – it also initiates the interpersonal assurance that the driver meant no harm and that he adheres to shared ethical values. Sometimes 'answering' may merely require a person to acknowledge his responsibility or to apologise. Thus, answerability, properly understood, is not identical to explainability[4] and does not require the answerable person to be able to give a particularly sophisticated or detailed report of what happened.[5]

So understood, this view on strict answerability differs, as I already explained in Part I, from the standard model in moral philosophy. My view differs 'extensionally' because it gives a different verdict on Williams's lorry driver case: unlike those other views, my view considers the lorry driver as morally answerable for the accident and the harm caused. And my view differs 'intensionally' because it gives an altogether different explanation of answerability. In my view, the condition of moral answerability is not the *reflection of judgement* but rather *agential causation*, ie that the person caused the harm which she was obliged to guard against.

[4] Kiener (2023) and Hubbs (2013) even argued that there can be answerability without an answer.

[5] Here, the driver is answerable despite his lack of fault. But this is not to deny that answerability is often an open-ended inquiry where it is unclear whether someone was at fault and where the certainty about the absence of fault, as simply assumed in the lorry driver case, is not a given.

Before I apply this notion of responsibility as strict moral answerability to AI, however, I shall provide an additional argument for its existence, given that most philosophers do not recognise it as a form of genuine moral responsibility.

A NOVEL ARGUMENT FOR STRICT MORAL ANSWERABILITY

In Part I, I defended strict moral answerability as a solution to the *Lorry Driver Paradox*. Now, I want to present another, independent argument so that my application of strict answerability to the context of AI need not rely on my previous, potentially controversial points. In particular, I argue that strict moral answerability can be supported by expanding on insights from John Gardner's work, in particular Gardner's view that when we fail to conform to reasons that apply to us, those reasons persist in exerting a certain normative force:

> If one does not fully conform to a reason – if one does not do exactly what it is a reason to do – the reason does not evaporate. It does not evaporate even though one was justified in not conforming to it. It does not evaporate even though it is now too late fully to conform to it. Instead it now counts as a reason for doing the next-best-thing. (Gardner 2005, 57)

In the first instance, reasons favour certain actions: a reason to take one's kids to the beach favours, trivially, taking one's kids to the beach. Whether we are also *required* to do so also depends, of course, on the presence or absence of countervailing reasons. However, as Gardner points out, if we fail to conform to our reasons, then – in the second instance – our reasons do not 'evaporate'. Rather, their demands are transformed into something else, namely into a demand for doing 'the-next-best-thing': having failed to take the kids to the beach today, we now ought to take them to the beach tomorrow or, if this is not possible, compensate them in some other way or at least apologise.

Here is why I think Gardner is right. When we do the next best thing, we strive to minimise our departure from the un-conformed-to reasons and express our recognition of the reasons we had in the first place. But most importantly, we thereby reaffirm our status as moral and rational agents, ie as beings to whom these reasons apply and who ought to conform to them as much as possible. Thus, if we think of ourselves as moral and rational agents, we cannot but accept the normative persistence of un-conformed-to reasons. *Qua* rational and moral agents, it is inconceivable that we could simply brush off non-conformity to reasons in the first instance and not aim to minimise our departure from their demands in the second.

I aim to build upon Gardner's insights and extend them to the situation of the lorry driver. In so doing, I shift the focus slightly. My primary concern goes beyond the general discussion of *reasons*, which was central to Gardner's account. Instead, I consider more specifically *prospective obligations* – namely those that pertain to guarding against types of harm. Moreover, I will also suggest a different reading of 'non-conformity'. I assume that the lorry driver met all reasonable expectations in attempting to prevent collisions with pedestrians. In this respect, he completely 'conformed to' his prospective obligations. However, there is another sense of non-conformity, which concerns the discrepancy between what the driver aimed to do with his precautionary measures on the one hand and the unfortunate outcome that occurred due to his bad luck on the other. Focusing on such cases, I ask what the 'next best thing' would be for the driver, or what it is that he morally ought to do after the accident.

To approach this question, it can help to identify first what the driver *must not* do – namely, dismiss the incident as mere bad luck and state that it has nothing to do with him. Andrew Cornford aptly describes such behaviour as 'callous' (Cornford 2011, 45), Wolf calls it 'appalling' (Wolf 2001, 12), and also Piovarchy critiques it sharply: 'If the driver … treats the child's death as simply unlucky and rejects any new duties, he displays a level of disregard for which we can blame him' (Piovarchy, 2020, 148).[6] We can blame the driver because such disregard constitutes disrespect and leads to what is known as 'expressive harm', ie harm which occurs when someone fails to respond appropriately after causing harm (*cf* Piovarchy 2020, 155–156). Thus, in exploring the normative aftermath of the lorry driver case, we can lead our general investigation into what the 'next best thing' for the driver is towards the more specific investigation into the actions required of the driver to avert disrespect and expressive harm.

This is where strict moral answerability becomes important. According to my view of strict answerability, the victim's parents are entitled to demand that the lorry driver answer for his role in the accident. They can demand that he acknowledge his involvement, explain the circumstances from his perspective, describe how he met or failed his responsibilities (such as taking precautionary measures), and that he provide assurances, such as restating his respect for the moral rights of others, reaffirming his commitment to shared ethical values, and helping the victims view the incident as a regrettable event rather than an act of negligence or disrespect.

In acknowledging and discharging his strict moral answerability, the driver finds a means of avoiding disrespect and averting expressive harm. To begin with, strict moral answerability allows the driver to recognise a shift in the relationship to the victim, respectively their family: while they might have been strangers prior to the accident, they are now connected by what happened in a very specific moral sense – one that requires second-personal recognition and thus opposes the sort of neglect inherent in disrespect. After all, answerability is itself a moral relationship between those who ought to provide an answer and those who are

[6] There is some divergence between Piovarchy and Gardner's account here. Whereas Piovarchy suggests that there may be *new* duties, Gardner may argue that the *old* duties are still there and now simply ask for the 'next best thing'. The debate as to whether there are new or old duties, respectively reasons, does not matter for my purposes. I shall only focus on the question of what people ought to do 'next' in cases like the lorry driver.

entitled to receive it. Moreover, strict moral answerability counteracts the harm asymmetry in the accident, ie the disproportionate allocation of harm to the victim,[7] by acknowledging an opposite asymmetry, ie one that gives the victim (or their family) the upper hand in terms of a certain right or entitlement to demand an answer from the driver. Thus, strict moral answerability can restore a potentially disrupted moral balance that could result in expressive harm. Finally, in fulfilling his strict moral answerability, the driver acknowledges that he owes something to the victim and their parents, and that he needs to comply with their requests for an explanation or justification. In so doing, he respects their dignity as persons and validates them – to use a phrase from J Rawls – as 'self-authenticating sources of valid claims' (Rawls 2005, 32, 96), ie beings who are not only entitled to assert claims on their behalf but also generate these claims themselves and are their primary originators, including claims to explanations and justifications. For these and other reasons, strict moral answerability is a key tool for the driver to avoid disrespect and expressive harm, and it thus outlines a core part of the 'next best thing' for the driver to do.

On this basis, I conclude that strict moral answerability is a key component of the moral aftermath of situations where we cause harm which we have an obligation to guard against. It is needed to avoid disrespect and avert expressive harm, and thus is core to, or at least part of, the 'next best thing' that the driver ought to do. For the same reason, it constitutes an important moral mechanism through which we navigate the complexities formed in the aftermath of harm. Thus, when we extend Gardner's initial ideas to Williams's lorry driver, we can conclude that the driver is morally answerable and, more precisely, that he is *strictly* morally answerable as no specific *mens rea* or fault was required. To be clear: this is not a knockdown argument. Rather, it is best understood as an inference to the best explanation. I propose strict moral answerability as the best account of the moral aftermath in cases like the lorry driver. Thus, we have reason to assert that strict moral answerability should form part of our responsibility framework.

This outline of, and support for, strict moral answerability completes the first half of this chapter. In the next section, I shall proceed and apply strict moral answerability to contexts of AI.

APPLYING STRICT MORAL ANSWERABILITY TO AI

Suppose it is no longer a lorry operated by a human driver, but rather an autonomous, AI-operated lorry that hits a pedestrian. Who would be responsible in this scenario? Is there anyone who resembles our lorry driver and satisfies the two clauses in my sufficient condition of strict moral answerability, ie the condition

[7] This is, of course, not to deny that the driver may suffer psychological trauma too.

that one is strictly morally answerable for some harm if one caused the harm (causation clause) and had an obligation to guard against such harm (obligation clause)?

By way of illustration, suppose there is a fatal accident with an autonomous vehicle, and many people across different stages of the vehicle's development and use played a role. Software engineers developed the algorithms that controlled the vehicle's motions, provided the integration of subsystems, and handled the sensor data fusion under rare environmental conditions. A quality assurance team conducted routine tests to simulate outlier scenarios which could expose AI system vulnerabilities in real-world settings. Regulatory compliance officers aimed to ensure that the AI-based software met existing standards and that these standards were updated to cover adequately the emerging technological complexities in autonomous vehicles. Users operated the vehicle, relied to varying degrees on the autonomous system, and maintained a certain, although potentially limited, level of alertness. User-experience designers created the interface that communicates the system status to users, thereby determining the number of potential alerts and influencing the driver's level of attention. Finally, safety consultants advised on risk assessment models that estimate the probability and impact of simultaneous system failures. Although this description remains an oversimplification, it already shows how much more complex the situation can be in the context of AI as compared to Williams's lorry driver case. Against this background, let us revisit the two conditions of strict moral answerability, building on the more general debates around causation and obligations, and introducing them to the debate on AI.

Causation

Symmetric Overdetermination

A first possibility of divergence between Williams's lorry driver and AI contexts is that, in the latter, we may encounter causal overdetermination. I assume that an outcome, eg some harm, is overdetermined if and only if two or more distinct and actual conditions are individually sufficient, but not necessary, for that outcome to occur (*cf* Funkhouser 2009; Sartorio 2012). By way of using a widespread example, suppose two assassins each fire a bullet and these hit the same victim simultaneously, leading to the victim's death. The victim's death would not have occurred in the absence of *both* bullets but would still have occurred if *either* bullet was fired without the other. This example is a special case of overdetermination, often called *symmetric* overdetermination, because (at least) two causes operate at the same time, creating a situation of, as Sara Bernstein puts it, 'double the causation' (Bernstein 2017, 170).

A similar scenario can occur in the context of AI. Consider Carol, who was the lead AI engineer in developing the neural networks and decision-making algorithms of a self-driving vehicle. Even though Carol exercised all the diligence that one could expect and tested the systems rigorously, an unexpected anomaly in the data-processing pipeline causes the vehicle to accelerate unexpectedly. Meanwhile, Dan, who operates the vehicle and is supposed to monitor its behaviour, as well as intervene if necessary, has set the system's driving parameters. However, Dan does not know that his specific configurations contribute to the acceleration of the vehicle in certain situations. Neither Carol's neural network nor Dan's settings are inherently flawed, nor do they make them culpable in any way – akin to the lorry driver's blamelessness in Williams's original example. Yet each of their actions independently suffices to cause the crash, which illustrates another case of symmetric overdetermination.

If we follow the previous description of such cases of overdetermination, understood as cases of 'double the causation', and apply my causation-clause, then *both* assassins as well as *both* Carol and Dan 'caused' the death. Therefore, (other things being equal) they are all also *fully* responsible for the outcome. But note the following important qualification, which Michael Zimmerman reminds us of:

> To say that someone is *fully* responsible is not to say that he is *solely* responsible; responsibility is not to be cut up, like a pie, so that the more people that join in a wrongdoing [or harming], the less responsibility to be allocated to each. On the contrary, responsibility may be multiplied. (Zimmerman 1985, 355, emphasis added)

Zimmerman's distinction between full and sole responsibility provides an important clarification of my view too. Whoever meets the causation clause of my view is on track to being *fully* responsible, yet there is no implication that they will be *solely* responsible as well. I endorse Zimmerman's rejection of the pie model of responsibility and argue that, in cases of symmetric overdetermination, many people can be responsible for the same event.

Moreover, Zimmerman later also provides a convincing rationale as to why this is a plausible view: the mere presence of other wrongdoers or causers of harm does not provide any excuse, exemption, justification or other responsibility-undermining explanation. Thus, the mere presence of other causing agents cannot affect one's responsibility either. Therefore, Carol and Dan are fully, yet not solely, responsible. They *share* responsibility in the sense where *shared* responsibility does not entail *distributed, or divided*, responsibility.

This conclusion is also further supported by some of my earlier considerations. After all, the situation Carol and Dan find themselves in significantly resembles that of the lorry driver. Like Williams's lorry driver, who faultlessly caused harm, Carol and Dan are similarly faultless. They, like the lorry driver, experience and may justifiably express agent-regret, are obliged to provide explanations and justifications for their actions to the victims of the accident upon request, and would cause disrespect and expressive harm if they denied the accident had anything to do with them. Consequently, Carol and Dan are strictly morally answerable for the accident, even though they find themselves in a situation of symmetric overdetermination, which was not the case in Williams's original lorry driver scenario. This conclusion would also hold if we added further participants. The number of symmetric overdeterminers does not matter (for the reasons outlined by Zimmerman) and therefore does not undermine the individual answerability of each of these causal overdeterminers.

Pre-emptive Overdetermination

Yet, there is also another type of overdetermination that may also arise in contexts of AI and therefore requires our attention, namely cases of *pre-emptive* overdetermination. Such cases are well illustrated by the canonical examples from Harry Frankfurt. In these examples, there is an evil neuroscientist who is prepared to interfere with an agent's brain and make her perform a certain act if the agent shows the slightest sign of not performing that very act on her own. Yet, as it happens, the agent performs the act independently and no interference is needed (Frankfurt 1969). This is a case of overdetermination because there are two distinct conditions, ie the agent's motivation and the neuroscientist's interference, which would be individually sufficient but not necessary for the outcome to occur. Yet, the neuroscientist does not actually *bring about* the outcome, but merely *guarantees* the outcome with his presence in the background (Funkhouser 2009, 350). The neuroscientist, unlike any of the two assassins or either Dan or Carol in my previous examples of symmetric overdetermination, only plays the role of a pre-empted backup rather than the role of a second operating cause.

Applying the causation clause of my view then leads to the conclusion that the pre-empted backup does not meet the causation clause and thus will not be responsible for what happens. After all, the pre-empted agent can resort to a so-called *denial:* the agent can simply state that she did not do the thing in question and thus avert responsibility. This is also the correct result: in Frankfurt's cases, it is the self-determining agent (rather than the non-interfering neuroscientist in the background) who is responsible for her own action. Thus, my view satisfactorily deals with cases of pre-emptive overdetermination. In such cases, only those agents who actually cause an outcome can be considered potential bearers of responsibility.

In the context of AI, pre-emptive overdetermination involving an autonomous vehicle could look as follows: Dan, the vehicle's operator or user, adjusts the control panel settings so that the AI will boost efficiency in traffic-navigation within a certain margin. Simultaneously, the software developer Carol designs an autonomous backup safety system, which is supposed to intervene if the other systems fail. Later, when the vehicle is in operation, a glitch in Dan's settings makes the vehicle speed up. However, had Dan's settings not caused the acceleration, a software malfunction in Carol's backup system would have done so. Thus, Carol's system is a pre-empted backup. Here, only Dan, not Carol, is comparable to Williams's initial lorry driver. Only Dan, not Carol, fittingly experiences and expresses agent-regret. Only Dan, not Carol, is obliged to answer to those who were harmed. And only Dan, not Carol, would be disrespectful and cause expressive harm if he did not answer to the demands for an explanation and justification. Thus, strict moral answerability would only be with Dan, not Carol.

Hence, dealing with cases of overdetermination in the context of AI requires that we distinguish between *symmetric* overdetermination, where all causing agents are responsible, and *pre-emptive* overdetermination, where only those who *bring about* an outcome, but not those who merely *guarantee* an outcome, are responsible.

Joint Causation

Now, consider joint causation: an outcome, eg some harm from AI, is jointly caused if and only if two or more distinct and actual conditions are jointly sufficient and individually necessary for that outcome to occur (as contrasted with overdetermination where the conditions are *individually* sufficient but not necessary). For example, suppose there are two assassins again, each firing a bullet at the same victim, but this time *both* bullets are required to kill the victim; either bullet on its own would be insufficient. Bernstein provides a good slogan for such cases when she says: 'Joint causation is often thought of as a kind of "causal teamwork", whereas overdetermination is often thought of as "double the causation"' (Bernstein 2017, 170). Thus, the relation between each assassin and the outcome is now different: whereas they individually *caused* the outcome in cases of symmetric overdetermination, they now only make a *causal contribution* to the outcome. This change requires that we reconsider each assassin's responsibility, and by extension the responsibility of people developing and using AI systems insofar as their situation is also one of joint causation.

In fact, cases of joint causation seem most prevalent in the context of AI, where the partial contributions of developers and users may accumulate and jointly cause harmful outcomes. Here is a possible scenario in the context of autonomous vehicles: A crash occurs due to at least two interdependent factors, each of which was necessary but only jointly sufficient. Our lead AI engineer, Carol, implements an enhancement to the vehicle's software, instructing it to accelerate when sensors detect clear road conditions, leveraging sophisticated techniques rooted in reinforcement learning and Markov Decision Processes. However, this functionality relies on confirmation from the vehicle's control settings to activate. Meanwhile, the vehicle owner, Dan, adjusts the control settings to handle ambiguous situations while maintaining a cautious approach unless explicitly signalled otherwise by the software. During intermittent fog, Carol's software misinterprets a clearing in the fog as safe and this leads to an increase in speed. At the same time, Dan's settings, which normally reflect a cautious approach, now misinterpret this as a confirmation of clear conditions and make the vehicle accelerate aggressively. The fog quickly returns and a collision results. Neither the software update nor the control settings alone would have caused the acceleration; only their coincidence led to the crash.[8]

To evaluate responsibility in joint causation, Bernstein begins with what she calls an 'Intuitive Doctrine: you are only morally responsible for what you cause' (Bernstein 2017, 165).[9] Bernstein then adds the claim that 'if one is morally responsible only for the outcome that one causes, one should also only be morally responsible for the *part* or *proportion* of an outcome that one causes' (Bernstein 2017, 167). Bernstein says the latter claim is just a 'precisification' (Bernstein 2017, 167) of the *Intuitive Doctrine* and eventually leads us to the following principle:

> **Proportionality**. An agent's moral responsibility for an outcome is proportionate to her actual causal contribution to the outcome. (Bernstein 2017, 167)

Unfortunately, Bernstein's view conflates two importantly different aspects, namely 'causing part of an outcome' and 'partly causing an outcome'. Consider the second version of the two assassins scenario again. Each assassin partly causes one single, indivisible outcome, ie death, as opposed to each of them causing separate parts of a compound outcome. Bernstein's view (ie that 'one should … only be morally responsible for the *part* or *proportion* of an outcome that one causes' (Bernstein 2017, 167)) assumes the latter and is thus unable to explain how both assassins can share the responsibility for the *death*, rather than just bear individual responsibility for the specific wounds that their separate bullets cause.[10] On Bernstein's precisification-view, then, the object of responsibility could only ever be part of the victim's death. Yet, we are unable to identify a distinct 'part' of death and, what is more, this view fails to capture the fact that each individual assassin is responsible for the *entire death*, rather than just parts of it.

Although Bernstein's argument is flawed because of the conflation of 'causing part of an outcome' and 'partly causing an outcome', her conclusion, *Proportionality*, can be rescued. To see how, we need to use an insight from Kaiserman's work on responsibility and causation. Kaiserman stated a widely accepted principle, which he called *Individualism*:

> **Individualism**: An agent A's degree of responsibility for some outcome *o* is *fully grounded* in facts about A, *o* and the relations between them. (Kaiserman 2021, 3598)

Individualism has a restrictive dimension because it holds that a person's responsibility can only be affected by those three aspects which it is 'fully grounded in', namely 'A' (facts about that person), 'o' (the outcome this person is alleged

[8] An additional example of this sort is provided in Kiener (2025).

[9] For the purposes of this chapter, I sidestep challenges to this view in accounting for responsibility for omissions.

[10] See also Kaiserman (2016) on the notion of causal contributions to a single indivisible outcome.

to be responsible for), and 'r' (the relation between 'A' and 'o'). Accordingly, just adding further assassins or operating causes, as in my previous examples of symmetric overdetermination, would not affect people's responsibility. Thus, Kaiserman confirms my previous conclusion.

But *Individualism* also highlights an important difference between cases of symmetric overdetermination and cases of joint causation. The relation 'r' is different in these types of cases: people *fully cause* (r_1), an outcome in symmetric overdetermination, but only *causally contribute* (r_2) to an outcome in joint causation. Thus, if responsibility is grounded in r, and thus affected by r, someone's responsibility in a case of joint causation will differ from someone's responsibility in a case of symmetric overdetermination, and Bernstein's *Proportionality* offers a plausible explanation of how: 'An agent's moral responsibility for an outcome is proportionate to her actual causal contribution to the outcome' (Bernstein 2017, 167), where the causal contribution describes the relation 'r'.

But spelling out what being *proportionate* means, that is determining whether people are more or less responsible in cases of joint causation than in cases of symmetric overdetermination, proves to be a thorny issue. As Bernstein noted, the assessment of responsibility in cases of joint causation will depend on one's theory of causation (Bernstein 2017, 170 ff).

Suppose one subscribes to a so-called 'productive' theory of causation, according to which causing is transferring energy. According to this theory, the assassins, as well as Carol and Dan in our AI example, would transfer greater energy in cases of overdetermination than in cases of joint causation. The energy that each agent transfers in overdetermination cases is sufficient for the outcome, whereas the energy that each of them transfers in cases of joint causation is insufficient and only necessary. Hence, this suggests that each assassin's, as well as Carol's and Dan's, responsibility is reduced in cases of joint causation.

However, if one chooses a Lewisian 'counterfactual dependence' theory of causation, according to which causing requires difference-making in the counterfactual sense, then the agents in joint causation cases bear greater responsibility.[11] There is no counterfactual dependence between the death and either of the two individual shootings in overdetermination cases, or between the accident and either Carol's or Dan's action, whereas there is such counterfactual dependence in cases of joint causation.

Thus, Bernstein concludes: 'Whether the assassins in [cases of overdetermination] … bear more moral responsibility than those in [cases of joint causation] … depends on which causal concept one employs' (Bernstein 2017, 172). Therefore, the claim that one's responsibility is proportionate to

[11] See, eg, David Lewis (1973; 2000). There may be other, ie non-Lewisian, theories of counterfactual dependence, and these theories may have different implications. Yet, the main point stands: the implication for responsibility can depend on which theory of causation one accepts. Thanks to Matthew Braham for pressing me to clarify this point.

one's causal contribution does not yet tell us the exact degree of responsibility, but merely that there is a connection between responsibility and causal contribution, and that there is at least *some* responsibility in cases of joint causation.

Degrees of responsibility could mean different things, including degrees of blameworthiness (if there was a harmful or wrongful action) or the range of liabilities one acquires through one's responsibility. In this chapter, however, I am concerned with answerability. Answerability is a binary rather than scalar notion: one either is or is not answerable. Thus, even if a person's desert for blame or her range of liabilities vary according to her causal contribution, this will not change *the fact that* she is answerable. Yet, degrees of responsibility could be understood as making a person's obligation or reasons to answer for their conduct more or less stringent. Accordingly, a person with a higher degree of responsibility would have a stronger obligation or stronger reasons to comply with the demands for an explanation or justification than a person with a lower degree of responsibility. And higher degrees of responsibility may also make it appropriate to approach the person with such for an explanation or justification before approaching those with lower degrees. This leads to a two-fold conclusion: degrees of responsibility do not affect *that* a person is answerable but may change how *strong* a person's obligation or reasons to answer are.

This is also the correct ethical assessment. Recall the joint causation of Dan and Carol, and add as many other contributing causes as you wish, to come closer to the complex reality of AI development and use. Perhaps the imperfectly integrated sensors misinterpreted the environmental data, or the warning systems inadequately alerted the user, or the safety protocols failed to compensate, and so on. Each party involved in the chain that led to the accident – engineers, testers, regulators, users, designers and consultants – made an incremental contribution to the harmful outcome. Still, all people involved can fittingly experience and express agent-regret. They are also all obliged, upon request, to explain and justify their conduct to those who were harmed and who are entitled to an explanation. If the engineers, testers, regulators, users, designers and consultants simply walked away and denied involvement, they would engender disrespect and expressive harm, just as the lorry driver in Williams's original case would. Their indifference and refusal to answer would be a morally inappropriate response to what happened. Thus, the minuteness of a contribution does not preclude one's strict moral answerability in cases of accidents. Each participant, in reflecting on their role, must consider and answer to the question of how even minor oversights or decisions contribute to outcomes of vast ethical significance. Therefore, even though the role of the numerous people involved in the chain that led to the accident are very different from that of the initial lorry driver, this does not preclude the significant aspects relevant to strict moral answerability and the need to avoid disrespect and express harm persisting in both scenarios. Therefore, even if there is just a causal contribution, rather than full causation, this is enough to satisfy the causation-clause of strict moral answerability.

On this basis, that is, insofar as the causation clause of my view is concerned, I conclude that everyone involved in joint causation of harm can be responsible in the sense of strict moral answerability. However, there may be some variation in how strongly they are obliged to answer. Moreover, *pace* Bernstein, I argue that people can be answerable for a single, indivisible outcome to which they causally contributed, but not for only parts of some compound outcome.

This conclusion now allows me to specify my causation clause: it requires that a person cause *or* causally contribute to some outcome. This occurs in cases of (symmetric) overdetermination as well as in cases of joint causation. Therefore, insofar as the roles of the people involved in the use and development of AI systems resemble the roles of my protagonists in the examples of symmetric overdetermination or joint causation, the AI developers (potentially very many) will bear responsibility as answerability for a harmful outcome.

Now that I have discussed the causation condition, I shall proceed to the obligation clause of my view.

Obligations

All people involved in the development and use of AI have the obligation to guard against certain types of harm, eg that the autonomous car hits a pedestrian, that the hiring algorithm unlawfully discriminates against certain applicants, or that the medical AI misdiagnoses patients. Thus, I shall assume that everyone involved in the development and use of AI shares an obligation of this general character, namely, the obligation to guard against the risks normally associated with an activity.

But to discharge this general obligation, different people may also be required to do different things, given their different involvement in the development and use of AI. For instance, consider once again the context of autonomous driving. Programmers and software engineers are obliged to implement suitable redundancies and fail-safes in the AI systems and thereby enable them to anticipate and mitigate potential failures under unexpected conditions. Quality assurance engineers are obliged to conduct extensive and rigorous testing that includes atypical scenarios to ensure system reliability and safety in real-world applications. Regulatory compliance officers are obliged to keep abreast of technological advancements and update safety regulations accordingly so that they reflect the capabilities and risks associated with the state of the art. Users of autonomous vehicles have an obligation to operate these vehicles only within prescribed limits and to maintain alertness to take control whenever necessary. User-experience designers are obliged to create clear, intuitive interfaces that effectively communicate the system's status and potential risks, ensuring that users can make informed decisions as quickly and as easily as possible. Safety consultants have an obligation to develop detailed risk assessments that consider not only typical but also rare scenarios. Corporate executives are also obliged to attach adequate importance to ethical considerations and safety in their business practices so that commercial goals will not compromise important ethical values and principles in the context of autonomous driving. This shows that all these obligations depend on the specific role one plays in the development and use of some AI system, as well as on the specific skillset one either has or can be expected to have in relation to guarding against certain types of harm.

Taking these points together, I assume that everyone in the development and use of AI shares the general obligation to guard against certain risks of harm and that they possess some more specific obligations, tailored to their position and expertise. What is important, however, is that all these obligations concern specific types of harm, rather than an obligation not to cause harm, without further qualification. Thus, whenever people cause or causally contribute to harm that they have an obligation to guard against, either an obligation shared with many others or an obligation specific to their role, they are strictly morally answerable.

This position leads to a two-fold result. On the one hand, the obligation clause specifies who is responsible for the harm caused by AI. My view identifies those people with specific (often role-based) obligations to guard against certain types of harm as meeting the sufficient condition of strict moral answerability and thus being eligible bearers of responsibility. On the other hand, the shared general obligation to guard against certain types of harm, such as autonomous cars hitting people, as well as the existence of further versatile role obligations, make it likely that many people in the development and use of AI will meet the obligation clause of my proposed view.

In conclusion, then, many people will meet the condition for strict moral answerability when AI causes harm: they meet the causation clause (either by causing or causally contributing) and they meet the obligation clause (by possessing various general and specific obligations to guard against certain types of harm). Thus, whenever a self-driving car causes an accident, or some other AI system causes harm, many of those involved in the development and use of this AI system are likely to become strictly morally answerable for the harmful outcome.

Thus, I arrive at the main idea of this chapter: in the context of AI, we do not face a responsibility *gap*, we face responsibility *abundance*.[12]

RE-INTERPRETING THE CHALLENGE FROM RESPONSIBILITY AND AI

This change of perspectives, ie from a responsibility gap to responsibility abundance, does not mean that the challenge concerning responsibility and AI

[12] Note that those who reject causation as a condition of responsibility may face an even greater abundance of responsibility in the context of AI, as they could include people with relevant obligations, even if they are outside the causal chain. These cases are beyond the scope of this chapter, but they show how my view about a responsibility abundance could apply in other types of case too, which could prove even more significant for the context of AI.

disappears. In fact, the abundance of responsibility is a problem on its own. Once numerous agents are responsible, it becomes impractical to hold all of them responsible. In practice, we simply lack the means to hold everyone answerable. But at the same time, we cannot just single some of them out because doing so would be arbitrary and unjust. Therefore, with responsibility abundance there is a dilemma: (i) the great number of agents makes it unfeasible to hold everyone responsible; and (ii) just singling some of them out would be arbitrary or unjust. In other words, it seems that we *cannot* do (i) and we *should not* do (ii). Thus, whereas the problem with a responsibility *gap* is that we lack what we want, the problem with responsibility *abundance* is that we cannot use what we have.

Reframing the challenge about responsibility and AI in terms of an abundance of responsibility offers several advantages, two of which are especially noteworthy. First, there is a *dialectic* advantage: the dilemmatic structure focuses our attention and highlights specific means to tackle the problem, ie address one of the two horns of the dilemma and establish answerability as a feasible and just social practice. This more specific description of the challenge contrasts with a rather hazy understanding of why a responsibility gap is a problem in the first place. While many address responsibility gaps, only very few attempt to explain why it is a serious problem, and some even argue that it is not problematic (Danaher 2022; Königs 2022). Thus, my proposal allows us to circumvent the ambiguity of the challenge's nature and also highlights specific ways to address it.

Second, there is a *theoretical* advantage: my proposal provides more robust grounds for a new way of thinking about responsibility, including ideas about 'taking responsibility'. Enoch and I argued that there is a normative power of taking responsibility, ie the ability to make oneself responsible for something by mere declaration (Enoch 2012; Kiener 2022). One of Enoch's central examples is Williams's lorry driver, who is not responsible immediately after the accident but can, and ought, to take responsibility by an act of will or declaration. I developed this idea too, and I claimed that suitably positioned people can make themselves responsible for the harm caused by AI simply by declaration. However, the strongest objection against such views is that responsibility cannot be created out of the blue. Just saying 'I hereby make myself responsible' does not automatically confer responsibility where it previously did not exist. It is at this point that my proposal in this chapter can intervene and provide another potential reply. The proposal in this chapter could show that there has always been some responsibility, ie strict moral answerability. Accordingly, taking responsibility need not be understood as creating responsibility *ex nihilo* but rather as making it possible for others to hold one responsible without having to contend with horn (ii) of the aforementioned dilemma and thereby acting unjustly. Thus, my proposal allows us to understand in a different way the normative change brought about by the act of taking responsibility, namely by giving others permission to hold one answerable without running into arbitrariness or injustice. So understood, this chapter's approach facilitates new theoretical grounds for more constructivist thinking about responsibility, where some forms of moral responsibility can be taken and negotiated, and not only simply discovered like a brute moral fact.

But before I conclude, I also need to address an objection. Some may still be unconvinced by the responsibility abundance. They may think that strict moral answerability is not genuine moral responsibility (Shoemaker 2013), or that even if strict moral answerability is genuine moral responsibility, there is still a lack of other types of responsibility, most notably those types associated with blame; and either way, responsibility gaps persist.

In response, I want to emphasise that a responsibility gap implies two aspects: first, the *absence* of responsibility and, second, the *need* for responsibility. Mere absence is not enough as, for example, we would not talk about responsibility gaps regarding the movements of the planets; we simply do not expect there to be any human responsibility involved here. But with the development of new technologies, such as AI, things are different: we imply that there must be some kind of responsibility, otherwise something is missing.

On the basis of this bi-partite structure of the claim about the responsibility gap (ie the absence of responsibility and the need for responsibility), there are also two corresponding ways of denying a responsibility gap: denying the *absence* of responsibility or denying the *need* for responsibility. My proposal could target both aspects. So far, I have presented my view as the claim that strict moral answerability is genuine moral responsibility, and I thereby denied the *absence* of moral responsibility. But in addition, and independently, my proposal could also be interpreted as showing that strict moral answerability (whether *genuine* moral responsibility or not) precludes the *need* for any other types of moral responsibility. This is because, once we manage to establish a feasible and just scheme of holding each other (strictly) answerable (see chapter ten), this will be a powerful tool for the socially sustainable use of AI. It is a scheme premised on mutual recognition, equality and respect. It is capable of creating and maintaining social trust in the development and use of technologies, and it encourages due diligence and inclusivity. If this is so, it is not clear what roles or functions other types of responsibility, especially those associated with blaming or punishing people, could have. It is unclear why we would still *need* blame and other forms of responsibility whenever there is strict answerability.

Thus, what started as an objection to my proposal – ie that the responsibility gap persists – is now reframed as a serious challenge addressed to the responsibility gap theorists. This challenge is to explain not only how strict moral answerability cannot be classed as genuine moral responsibility or why it excludes other types of moral responsibility, but also why there is a real need for other types of moral responsibility, *after* we have established a scheme of strict moral answerability. Unless this challenge is addressed, the defence of responsibility gaps is incomplete.

CONCLUSION

This chapter proposed a change of perspective, from responsibility gaps to responsibility abundance. I explained and defended the idea of strict moral answerability, and then applied it to the context of AI. My proposed change of perspective offers dialectic and theoretical advantages: it allows us to address the challenge posed by responsibility and AI with greater precision and it breaks new ground for thinking about responsibility. So understood, framing the challenge in terms of a responsibility abundance promises to overcome some of the main obstacles in the current debate and helps us to gain a fresh perspective on responsible AI.

Hence, strict moral answerability is a valuable proposal, not only in the context of general moral responsibility and the *Lorry Driver Paradox*, but also in the more specific setting of artificial intelligence. However, it should be noted that strict moral answerability is not a self-standing solution in the context of AI. Rather, it poses a new challenge. At the end of Part I, I claimed that the normative power of taking responsibility might help in situations where there is an abundance of responsibility (understood as answerability). For this reason, I shall now continue to investigate the normative power of taking responsibility in the context of AI, first in isolation, and later with an eye to combining it with the idea of strict moral answerability.

8

*Closing AI's Responsibility Gap at Will**

As I MENTIONED earlier, there is a controversial debate over whether AI creates 'responsibility gaps', ie situations in which no one is morally responsible for the harm caused by AI.[1] Some scholars have argued that the use of AI creates responsibility gaps (Matthias 2004; Sparrow 2007; Danaher 2016; De Jong 2020) precisely because it removes control and understanding, whereas others have denied the existence of such gaps (Johnson 2015; Himmelreich 2019; Tigard 2020). Still others have endorsed an intermediate position, arguing that gaps exist but that they are narrower than usually imagined (Schulzke 2013; Simpson and Müller 2016; Nyholm 2020, ch 3).

In this chapter, I shall set aside my results from the previous chapter and assume – for the sake of argument – that at least some of the most sophisticated AI systems do create responsibility gaps. In so doing, I can take an impartial point of view and ask whether we can bridge these gaps *at will*, viz whether we can *take responsibility* for AI-caused harm simply by performing a certain speech act, such as communicating the intention of hereby making oneself responsible, which I understand to be analogous to how people give permission for something (via consent) simply by communicating the intention of hereby giving a permission. So understood, taking responsibility would be a genuine 'normative power'. Thus, if this normative power exists, people could simply *make* themselves morally responsible for something they would otherwise not be responsible for. I will argue that a certain form of such a normative power does indeed exist, and I thereby aim to address not only a pressing challenge in current AI ethics but also to shift some of the central paradigms in the debate on moral responsibility more generally.

I will proceed as follows: I will first discuss and reject the view of Marc Champagne and Ryan Tonkens (henceforward 'CT'), who advocate a view of *taking liability* in the context of military AI (where liability designates a certain type of responsibility distinct from answerability). According to this view, a military commander can and must, ahead of time, accept liability to blame and punishment for any harm caused by autonomous weapon systems under her command. I will then defend my own proposal of *taking answerability*,

* Large parts of this chapter were first published in the journal *Ethical Theory and Moral Practice*, as an open access publication. See Kiener (2022).

[1] For other formulations of what a 'responsibility gap' is, see Himmelreich (2019) and List (2021).

viz the view that people can make themselves morally answerable for the harm caused by AI systems, not only ahead of time, but also when harm has already been caused. Finally, I will outline the extent to which the normative power of taking answerability can close AI's responsibility gaps and also explain how my account can remain attractive even to those who deny the existence of genuine responsibility gaps.

Applied to the *Autonomous AI Conundrum*, this solution could be presented as follows, parallel to the solution from chapter three:

1* **Initially,** the users and developers of the AI-powered car are not morally responsible for the person's death.
2* *Apology Principle*: one ought to apologise only if one is morally responsible for a certain harm.
3*** Someone among the users or developers of the AI-powered car ought to **take responsibility and, having done so, subsequently also** apologise.

Before I proceed, let me clarify two aspects. First, the only responsibility gap that can be addressed by means of a normative power will be the gap concerned with responsibility as answerability, rather than responsibility as liability to blame or punishment. Second, even in addressing the responsibility-as-answerability gap, the effect of the proposed normative power may be limited in the end.

CHAMPAGNE AND TONKENS' (CT'S) PROPOSAL: THE NORMATIVE POWER OF TAKING PROSPECTIVE LIABILITY

Outline of CT's View

CT focus on AI in military contexts, especially on autonomous weapon systems, and they accept that those systems create responsibility gaps (or 'vacuums' as they also call them). Gaps arise, they argue, because '(1) a programmer [or any other human person in the development and use of the AI] cannot be justifiably held responsible for the actions of a truly autonomous robot and … (2) holding a nonsentient robot responsible is meaningless and unsatisfactory' (Champagne and Tonkens 2015, 134). However, CT still claim that 'there is a way to seal the responsibility vacuum' (Champagne and Tonkens 2015, 126). More precisely, they argue for

> the possibility of 'blank check' responsibility: A person (or persons) of sufficiently high military or political standing could accept responsibility for the actions (normal or abnormal) of all autonomous robotic devices – even if that person could not be causally linked to those actions besides this prior agreement.' (Champagne and Tonkens 2015, 126)

And they add: 'we regard it as fair and reasonable for the commanding officer to willingly and freely assign responsibility to herself, ahead of time' (Champagne and Tonkens 2015, 133).

Thus, CT argue that a person can *accept* or *take* responsibility for something they would otherwise not be responsible for. It is a person's act of will or communication that creates this person's responsibility for AI-caused harm in the first place. CT call such a taking of responsibility 'noncausal imputation' (Champagne and Tonkens 2015, 127, 136) and describe it as entering into an 'explicit social contract' (Champagne and Tonkens 2015, 136). So understood, taking responsibility is a *normative power*: a person takes responsibility for something simply by performing a certain speech act, just as a person gives permission for something simply by performing the act of consent.

More specifically, CT talk about taking *prospective* responsibility rather than *retrospective* responsibility. In other words, people take responsibility only 'ahead of time', viz for harm that certain AI systems may cause in the future, but not for harm that has already been caused.

In addition, CT talk about responsibility in terms of *liability to blame and punishment*. To take responsibility, they explain, is 'to accept blame (or praise) for whatever robotic acts transpire in war' (Champagne and Tonkens 2015, 132), to become 'liable to receive blame for any self-initiated robot acts deemed immoral' (Champagne and Tonkens 2015, 132), and – as a result – to be 'subject to punishment' (Champagne and Tonkens 2015, 134) for the robots' harmful actions.

Finally, CT argue that certain people, ie the 'suitably ranked and sufficiently informed person or (persons)' (Champagne and Tonkens 2015, 133), are not only *able* to, but also *have* to, take responsibility. In other words, it is 'a nonnegotiable condition for accepting the position of authority' (Champagne and Tonkens 2015, 132) of, say, the most highly ranked military commander or the politician in charge of a military operation, that these people also take responsibility, ahead of time, for 'whatever robotic acts transpire in war' (Champagne and Tonkens 2015, 132). CT do not specify who else might be *able* to take responsibility for robotic acts, eg whether the remote computer programmer might be able to do so too, but they are clear that certain people *must* take responsibility.

Summarising these points, we can see that CT present an account of taking *prospective blame*-responsibility as a *non-negotiable condition* of certain positions of authority, like the position of military commander. To support their view, CT present two main arguments. First, they claim that we already accept something like taking responsibility by an act of will in the realm of medical consent:

> It is standard to use informed consent as part of our gauge of the ethics of intersubjective practices (e.g. patient recruitment for experimental research), and with such consent in place, (at least some) responsibility is thereby transferred to the agent doing the consenting. (Champagne and Tonkens 2015, 133)

CT here argue that medical consent not only creates permission but also shapes responsibility. When a patient consents to a medical procedure, he not only permits his physician to proceed but also takes responsibility for the risks inherent in the medical procedure; in other words, the patient foregoes the right to complain if certain risks materialise, at least as long as the medical procedure is performed consistently with professional standards.[2] In a similar way, they argue that people can take responsibility, or can consent to taking responsibility, in the context of AI too.

Second, CT claim that we also already take responsibility when accepting new roles. For instance, when accepting a job at a university, I impose on myself certain obligations concerning teaching, administration and research that I would otherwise lack. CT argue that the idea that a military commander could take responsibility when accepting the role of commander is very similar. Thus, CT present their proposal as a combination and further development of two already accepted ideas, ie the idea that consenting can imply taking responsibility and the idea that we take responsibility when assuming new roles.

Criticism of CT's View

CT present an intriguing proposal. Yet, their proposal faces two dilemmas and, therefore, we ought to reject it.

Dilemma 1: Either Blame is Inappropriate or CT's Normative Power is Redundant

In CT's view, when a military commander takes responsibility, the commander will have to accept 'blame' (Champagne and Tonkens 2015, 132) and be 'subject to punishment' (Champagne and Tonkens 2015, 134) for the robots' actions, eg the unlawful killing of non-combatants. Yet, the military commander may still be without fault. What is more, it is precisely in such cases of faultless causation of harm where CT's 'blank check'-responsibility is supposed to close the arising responsibility gaps.

But how could others genuinely *blame* the commander without implying fault? As Miranda Fricker explained: 'blame is out of order when one does bad things through no fault of one's own. If no fault, then no appropriate blame' (Fricker 2016, 170). In Gary Watson's view, 'to blame (morally) is to attribute something to a (moral) fault in the agent' (Watson 2004, 266). And Wolf says that blame concerns 'judgments and attitudes we may form in response to faulty behavior' (Wolf 2011, 332). Thus, one cannot fittingly 'blame' another person when that person is faultless, and a mere declaration to accept blame cannot make a difference either. Hence, if there is to be genuine blame, there must be fault too.

[2] For a discussion of this point in the context of medical AI, see also Kiener (2021, 710).

The rationale behind this position is that, conceptually speaking, we cannot distinguish moral blame from, say, sadness or disappointment without indicating that blame registers (at least perceived) moral fault in its target. If, as *cognitive* theories of blame hold (Watson 1996; Hieronymi 2004), blame is essentially a negative moral judgement about a person or her conduct, then such a judgement requires referring to some moral fault, or otherwise it could not hold up its distinctive moral negativity. If, as *emotional* theories of blame hold (Shoemaker 2017; Menges 2017), blame essentially involves specific forms of emotional engagement, most notably resentment or anger, then some kind of moral fault in the addressee of blame is needed too, or otherwise anger and resentment become unfitting. Or if, as *conative* theories of blame hold, and in particular Scanlon's version (Scanlon 2008), blame registers some moral impairment to an interpersonal relationship, then we also need to refer to a moral fault in the blamed person, or otherwise it would become implausible why there is this moral impairment Scanlon has in mind, viz why someone would have reason to modify their relation to the blamed person by, for instance, not considering them a friend anymore (Scanlon 2008, 129). Hence, across these major approaches to blame, some reference to fault is required to make an account of blame not only *intensionally* adequate, ie provide a sound explanation of what blame *is* (as opposed to sadness or disappointment), but also *extensionally* adequate, ie provide an account that correctly separates blame from other similar, yet distinct reactions or judgements (such as sadness or disappointment).

Following these approaches to blame, I will assume that a person is 'at fault' when they committed a harmful or wrongful act, or omitted to perform some required act, without justification or excuse.[3] In other words, fault is the moral stain that results from conduct which is neither justified nor excused. So understood, fault may arise in a wide range of cases, potentially including cases where people act from a flawed character, even when they could not control their character. Yet, importantly, fault requires more than just doing something that causes harm, eg taking a risk that later materialises. This is because when, say, a military commander takes a risk in employing an autonomous weapon system, the commander could, in principle, be justified in doing so (if, after all, it was the best thing to do, all things considered) or be excused (eg because the commander was non-culpably ignorant of a crucial aspect of the situation). In either case, the commander would not be at fault, morally speaking, and not blameworthy, even though the risk materialised and harm was done. Cases where the commander is excused and faultlessly causes harm resemble Williams's famous example of the 'lorry driver who, *through no fault of his*, runs over a child' (Williams 1981, 28, emphasis added). Just like Williams's

[3] Due to the clause on omissions, note that fault does not require an actual causal link between an outcome and a specific act.

unlucky lorry driver, CT's unlucky commander may cause severe harm while intentionally engaging in a certain activity or taking a certain risk. Yet, both the driver and the commander may have displayed the utmost diligence and caused the harm through no fault of their own. But CT's account applies to such cases of faultless harming and demands that the commander be subjected to blame. What is more, as already mentioned, it is *precisely* in these cases of faultless harming where the responsibility gap arises and CT's account on 'blank check' responsibility purports to close it.

But once we clarified that blame presupposes fault, we can see that CT face a dilemma: either (i) blame is inappropriate in the absence of fault and, thus, the act of taking responsibility cannot extend liability to blame; or (ii) blame is appropriate in the presence of fault, but then the act of taking responsibility is redundant since appropriate blame tracks fault and not prior acts of taking responsibility at will. Either way, CT's view that one can make oneself liable to blame by an act of will is mistaken. One cannot fittingly 'blame' a faultless person, and a declaration to accept blame cannot make a difference either, just as one cannot fittingly hate someone merely because they declared themselves to be worthy of hate.

However, this objection to CT's proposal not only applies to the liability to *blame*, but also to the liability to *punishment*, since punishment is also connected to fault. As Duff explains:

> A criminal trial aims to determine whether someone accused of committing such a wrong is provably guilty; a conviction does not just record in neutral tones that the defendant committed the wrong without justification or excuse, but condemns or blames him for committing it. The punishment to which he is then normally sentenced communicates that blame to the offender and to others; this is part of what distinguishes criminal punishment from other kinds of burden that states can impose, and criminal law from other kinds of legal regulation. (Duff 2021, 1)

Thus, even when we think about (legal) punishment, rather than (moral) blame, a similar dilemma arises: either (i) punishment is inappropriate in the absence of fault and, thus, the prior act of taking responsibility cannot extend penal liability; or (ii) punishment is appropriate in the presence of fault, but then the act of taking responsibility is redundant, since appropriate punishment tracks fault and not the prior decision to extend one's penal liability. Thus, it seems that CT's focus on liability to blame and punishment creates a fundamental problem in their view, with regards to both moral blame and legal punishment.[4]

[4] I here agree with Marcus Schulzke, who also argues that commanders can be responsible for the harm caused by autonomous weapon systems. In Schulzke's view, and as in my view, the commanders' responsibility, understood as liability to blame (Schulzke 2013, 215, 216), does not depend – as CT claim – on an act of taking responsibility alone, but rather on the commanders' specific involvement in the use of AWS. As Schulzke elaborates: 'Commanders should be held responsible for sending the AWS into combat with unjust or inadequately formulated ROE [Rules of Engagement], for failing to ensure that the weapons can be used safely, or for using AWS to fight in unjust conflicts, as all of these

Dilemma 2: Either the Arguments from Strict Liability are Decisive against CT's Proposal or CT's Proposal cannot close Responsibility Gaps

However, CT might have a partial reply to my objections so far. Even if, in morality, there is no fault-free blame, in the criminal law there is the possibility of *strict* (ie blame-free) penal *liability*. Thus, could CT defend their view at least from this legal perspective?

By way of further elaboration, '[o]ffences of strict liability require proof that the defendant performed the prohibited conduct, but do not require proof that the defendant was blameworthy' (Herring 2020, 210). Applied to the commander: it would only need to be shown that the autonomous weapon system caused harm and thereby violated a legal norm when the commander was on duty, not that the commander was in any way blameworthy or at fault. However, I need to be clear at this point: the question concerning CT's proposal is not whether strict liability itself would be justified in cases of the harm caused by autonomous weapon systems. The question is, more specifically, whether military commanders could simply decide whether to impose such strict liability on themselves, ahead of time. But to address the latter question, we can still begin by considering the former question, ie the question about strict liability *per se*, and then evaluate how the related arguments change once we focus on the normative power of imposing strict liability, instead of traditional strict liability.

Support for strict liability *per se* is weak in the context of autonomous weapon systems because some of the key arguments against strict liability apply their full force. Firstly, strict liability offences normally concern

> 'less serious' offences [that] play the role of regulating people's behaviour so that society can work effectively, rather than indicating that the defendant has behaved in a morally reprehensible way. These regulatory offences often do not require proof of mens rea because they do not carry the weight of moral censure that more serious crimes carry. (Herring 2020, 211)

Yet, as CT claim, military commanders could be responsible for clear war crimes, such as the 'killing spree' (Champagne and Tonkens 2015, 125) of a robot which shoots 'clearly surrendering' (Champagne and Tonkens 2015, 128) people. Thus, to this extent, a strict liability offence is inappropriate in this context.

Second, in strict liability offences, the costs of dangerous activities are normally placed on those who stand to benefit most from them (Turner 2019, 91).

conditions that enable or constrain an AWS are controlled by the commanders' (Schulzke 2013, 215). In all these cases, Schulzke says, commanders are responsible *when and because* they did not take 'adequate precautions' (Schulzke 2013, 214) or showed 'negligence of not guarding against foreseeable dangers' (Schulzke 2013, 214). Thus, the grounds of blame-related responsibility have to involve at least 'negligence' (Schulzke 2013, 213, 214), if not recklessness, which means they have to involve fault. This is where Schulzke and I diverge from CT, who claim that an act of taking responsibility alone could ground liability to blame or punishment.

Yet, it is not the commander who would benefit most from the use of autonomous weapon systems. The commander uses those systems to protect human soldiers and engages in military action for her country. CT argue that military commanders receive '[s]ocial prestige' (Champagne and Tonkens 2015, 125) in their occupation. But the intricacies and numerous interests at stake in war are far too complex to assume that the use of autonomous weapon systems primarily benefits those deciding their use. Thus, to this extent, strict liability is inappropriate too.

Third, most strict liability offences do not carry a serious stigma and can therefore be justified (Carpenter 2003, 221–223; Herring 2020; see also *R v Hughes* [2013] 1 WLR 2461). Yet, killing innocent people would come with a serious stigma and, to this extent too, strict liability for the harms of autonomous weapon systems is inappropriate.

In light of these points, the case against strict liability *per se* seems decisive. But how do these arguments change if it is no longer a question of strict liability *per se* but rather one of a *normative power* to impose such strict liability on oneself, as CT suggest? It seems that the core of these arguments against strict liability is that strict liability imposes a serious burden on the person being held liable, eg an accusation of serious wrongdoing and stigma, without giving that person any meaningful control over whether they will be subject to such a burden. Introducing a normative power and prior agreement can mitigate this aspect: it is up to a person to decide whether or not to accept such strict liability in the future, eg it is the commander's decision whether to accept a certain role which involves the use of autonomous weapon systems, or whether to decline that role. Is this enough to save CT's proposal?

Unfortunately, introducing such a normative power does not provide sufficient control to mitigate the arguments against strict liability. According to CT's proposal, the commander would need to decide, ahead of time, whether to accept strict liability for *any* harm caused by autonomous weapon systems when she is on duty. But in this prior decision, the commander could not reasonably foresee what harm she is likely to become liable for. Moreover, the control the commander has is further limited by the fact that she can only exercise the normative power of taking responsibility *once*, namely when deciding whether to accept her role as a commander. As soon as she *is* the commander, there is no further possibility of taking or rejecting responsibility at will so that, *within the role of being a commander*, a person is strictly liable in the traditional sense. For this reason, CT's normative power does not give people significant control. It only provides the amount and the type of control that people already have in other areas where they can decide, ahead of time, whether to engage in certain activities to which the law attached strict liability.

But what if we drop the claim that military commanders must also, as a condition of accepting their role, accept strict liability ahead of time and we grant the commanders more discretion over whether to take responsibility *within* their role? This would create more control and depart from traditional models of strict liability. Unfortunately, however, this path would lead CT to a another dilemma: to mitigate the force of the standard arguments against strict liability (which seem decisive against CT's proposal), CT need to grant the military commander considerably more discretion over whether she will face strict liability; the greater the discretion, particularly within the role of being a commander, the less decisive these standard arguments against strict liability will be. But to close the responsibility gap, CT cannot grant any significant discretion at all, otherwise it would be completely contingent whether liability is taken. Thus, CT's proposal faces an insurmountable problem: they need to do both at once – ie both increase and decrease the discretion for the commander.

I therefore conclude that even the strict penal liability model is not a defensible version of CT's proposal. The major obstacle in CT's proposal is the focus on responsibility in terms of *liability*, either to moral blame or legal punishment. Thus, if we are to develop a better version of a normative power of taking responsibility, this is where change is needed.

MY PROPOSAL: THE NORMATIVE POWER OF TAKING RETROSPECTIVE ANSWERABILITY

To make a fresh start, I will now move the focus away from responsibility, understood as liability to blame and punishment, to responsibility, understood as moral answerability. I continue to endorse my definition of answerability from this book, which I have borrowed from Angel Smith. So understood, moral answerability (henceforward 'answerability') can also come with an obligation to answer and explain harmful conduct – normally one's own – and thereby respond to those who have the standing to demand such an explanation. Moral answerability may also lead to further obligations, such as the obligation to apologise, to follow up on the well-being of those who have been harmed, to take precautionary measures so that similar harm will not recur, and so on. This list is not exhaustive but shows that answerability, as I understand it, can be associated with a certain set of obligations linked to moral responsibility.

In what follows, I will rely on this notion of answerability and argue that, under certain circumstances, there exists a normative power of making oneself morally answerable in this way, both prospectively and retrospectively, for the harm caused by sophisticated AI systems.[5] I will present two main arguments for this view, both of which go beyond my claims from Part I and thus provide

[5] So far, I have assumed that taking responsibility requires the performance of an explicit speech act. In formal contexts such as the military, this assumption seems justified. However, my proposal can remain open to the possibility that people may take responsibility in ways other than performing an explicit speech act. For instance, in informal contexts, a person might take responsibility simply by apologising. See for instance Enoch (2012).

further additional support in favour of a normative power to take responsibility. They are meant as additional support independent of the significance of the normative power of taking responsibility to solving the *Lorry Driver Paradox*.

Argument 1: Analogy to Promises

Owens argues that the normative power of 'promising exists because it serves our *authority interest*' (Owens 2012, 146). In this section, I extend Owens's view on promising to support the normative power of taking responsibility too. More specifically, I claim that, if we accept at least the outline of Owens's influential view on promising, we should also accept my specific view on taking responsibility as answerability.

Authority interests, Owens explains, are *normative* interests, viz interests in normative aspects, such as the existence of certain moral obligations. More specifically, authority interests are 'interests in *controlling* what others are obliged to do' (Owens 2012, 142; emphasis added). Promises serve those authority interests because when I receive and accept a promise, I gain control over a particular moral obligation that another person owes to me. As the promise-receiver, I can now decide whether to release you from your promise and thereby control whether you are morally obliged to act as promised. Such control is valuable because it can balance power-asymmetries in personal relationships (since the promise-giver transfers some of their control over the situation to the promise-receiver), it can create morally valuable relationships (since promising may express a commitment to another person's needs), it can assist social co-ordination and, as Shiffrin argues, it is key to intimate relationships such as friendships or the parent-child relationship (Shiffrin 2008). Therefore, Owens concludes: 'it is *good* for people to have authority, that the simple possession of authority over certain matters makes their lives go better (*ceteris paribus*). The normative force of a promise derives from this fact about human well-being' (Owens 2012, 150).

However, Owens's account does not stop at the interests of the *promise-receiver* (the promisee). The rationale behind the normative power of promising also includes the interests of the *promise-giver* (the promisor). As Owens explains:

> [W]e all have an interest in being able to satisfy the needs of others should we so wish. Where the promisee has an interest in acquiring authority over the promisor, the promisor often has an interest in being able to grant this authority, an interest in having the power to make promises. (Owens 2012, 146)

In other words, if – as receivers of promises – we have important authority interests, then – as givers of promises – we also have an interest in being able to satisfy others' authority interests, since the power to satisfy the important interests of others can be a vital asset in our lives, especially when it comes to forming and maintaining valuable personal relationships. Thus, Owens explains that the normative power exists because it serves the important authority interests of those receiving promises, as well as the correlated interests of those being able to satisfy these authority interests.

I will now devise an argument similar to Owens's to support the normative power of taking responsibility. More precisely, I will claim that there is a so-called *answerability interest*, and that the *answerability interest* is to *taking responsibility* what the *authority interest* is to *promising*, so that, if we accept that authority interests ground the normative power of promising, we should also accept that answerability interests ground the normative power of taking responsibility.

Answerability interests, like authority interests, are *normative* interests, viz interests in normative aspects, such as the existence of certain moral obligations. More specifically, answerability interests are, like authority interests, interests in *controlling* those moral obligations. Yet, answerability interests do not concern the moral obligations we receive through promises, but rather the moral obligations that arise with moral answerability. Earlier, I defined moral answerability as an obligation to answer and explain, and I claimed that such answerability also leads to further obligations, such as the obligation to follow up on those who have been harmed, the obligation to apologise and thereby acknowledge the moral significance of the harm, or the obligation to take precautionary measures to prevent similar future events. Thus, I understand answerability interests as interests in the *existence of* and in *one's control over* the moral obligations connected to the moral answerability of others.

So described, we can see why answerability interests are important. When we suffer harm through other people's action, we have an interest that *some* people not only plan to or *de facto* explain to us what happened, follow up on us, etc, but also that they *morally owe* this to us. The existence of such moral obligations is important because, when other people have these obligations, this signifies that our having been harmed is not just some natural misfortune or a case of a damaged object, ie something to be filed in an insurance company's drawer, but rather something that requires interpersonal moral acknowledgment. Moreover, it is important to us that we can also control those moral obligations of others by deciding whether or not to release them from these obligations, just as it is important for us to control others' obligations in this way in the context of promising. This is because such control lifts us from the status of mere *patients*, viz those who suffered harm, to that of genuine (moral) *agents*, viz those who have an active say in the moral aftermath of the harm. Being denied this active role would degrade us, objectify us, and insult our status as being worthy of respect.

Normally, our answerability interests are satisfied because human-induced harm normally comes with some people's moral answerability anyway. Yet, sometimes our answerability interests may remain unsatisfied. If AI really creates responsibility gaps, then there is a human-induced harm without moral answerability, which leaves our answerability interests frustrated.[6] It is only the normative power of taking responsibility at will, viz the power to impose moral answerability on oneself, that could create moral answerability and thereby satisfy the answerability interests of those who have been harmed. Thus, just as only the normative power of *promising* can serve some of our *authority interests*, only the normative power of *taking responsibility* can serve some of our *answerability interests*.

But it is not just about the interests of the people being harmed – it is also about the interests of everyone else, and in particular those who have been involved in the causation of harm. Some of the latter, even if they are not morally responsible (judged by the facts of the situation), may be in a unique position to *take* responsibility. If they do, they can provide comfort to those who have been harmed and help them overcome their distress and suffering. What is more, if a person freely imposes on himself the moral obligations and burdens associated with answerability in order to help others (when that person would otherwise not be morally answerable), he displays virtue. In taking responsibility, a person acts like the generous person described by Wolf and Jordan MacKenzie, viz a person who 'voluntarily benefits or tries to benefit others at cost to herself' (Wolf 2001, 14), refusing to be a person who is 'more concerned with saving face than helping others' (MacKenzie 2017, 110). Thus, just as Owens explains that authority interests are not only significant for those who possess them but also for those who can satisfy them, I claim in a similar way that answerability interests are not only significant for those harmed parties who possess them but also for those who can satisfy them. Satisfying answerability interests provides a chance to benefit others, to form valuable moral relationships, and to develop one's moral excellence.

Hence, to come full circle: the normative power of taking responsibility satisfies answerability interests when they would otherwise be left unsatisfied, just as the normative power of promising serves authority interests when these would otherwise be left unsatisfied. Therefore, we can support the normative power of taking responsibility in the context of AI in a similar way to Owens's original account of promising: just as authority interests ground the normative power of promising, answerability interests ground the normative power of taking responsibility.

This Owens-style argument also sharpens the contour of this normative power of taking responsibility. To begin with, this argument specifically supports the focus on responsibility as *answerability*, rather than liability. Since the interests of the person *taking* responsibility are equally important in this argument, and not just the interests of the person being harmed, a normative power of taking liability could not be sufficiently supported. After all, as

[6] Examples include autonomous weapon systems killing civilians, surgical robots paralysing patients, or autonomous cars injuring pedestrians.

argued in my critique of CT's proposal, there are strong objections against strict liability in cases of responsibility gaps, and such objections receive their force from not taking sufficient account of the interests of the person subject to liability.[7]

In addition, my Owens-style argument would include the power of taking *retrospective* responsibility, viz taking responsibility for a harmful event, even if it has already occurred. I hereby differ from CT, who only focus on taking *prospective* responsibility, viz taking responsibility for things in the future. Retrospective responsibility is included because answerability interests apply equally in cases in which harm has already occurred: even if it has already occurred, those harmed still have equal, or even stronger, answerability interests in the existence of moral answerability. Yet, taking *prospective* answerability will remain significant too.

Furthermore, my argument suggests that not everyone *can* take responsibility. I claimed that taking responsibility is grounded in answerability interests. But if so, the power of taking responsibility must also be limited to those who can, at least in some basic way, satisfy others' answerability interests. To do so, I claim, one must have been involved in the use or development of the AI system that caused harm. This is because being involved in the harm not only puts one in a special position to explain what happened, but also because one's involvement is a condition of responding meaningfully to those who have been harmed. After all, if I were to claim responsibility for some AI-related harm to which I have no connection at all, the victims of the harm may understandably perceive such conduct as completely unrelated to them, and perhaps even as insulting or as an attempt to divert attention away from those who should take responsibility instead. Thus, the power of making oneself morally answerable for the harm caused by an AI-system is restricted to those who have been involved in the development and use of that AI.

But before I proceed, a few clarifications are in order. First, the type of involvement in the development and use of AI that I am concerned with is still insufficient to ground responsibility on its own, since I continue to assume that there is a responsibility gap. Second, such involvement can take place at different stages, as my phrase 'involvement in the *development and use* of AI' indicates. For instance, someone could be involved as a computer scientist in the development of an AI system or as an end-user in the final application. Third, involvement can be usefully analysed in terms of two important metrics. The first is *proximity*, ie the temporal or spatial distance between an agent's conduct and the AI-related outcome. End-users normally show greater proximity to an

[7] This is not to say that the people harmed might not have some 'retributivist interests' as (Danaher 2016) put it, viz an interest in seeing someone punished for the harm. But since these interests would mainly reside with the people harmed, and not extend to those being punished, such interests are unlikely to contribute to an Owens-style argument that includes the interests of all parties involved.

outcome than the computer scientists who developed the system. The second metric is *relevance*, which concerns the importance of a person's involvement. Here, the computer scientists could sometimes have made a more important contribution to the AI's outcome than the end-user, at least when the latter uses the system only for its previously determined purpose. These two metrics are particularly useful in settings with multiple agents, as in the context of AI, and can help to identify where taking responsibility has its greatest value. The greater the proximity (to the outcome) and relevance (of the contribution), the more likely it is that a person can satisfy an answerability interest and, thus, the higher the value of this person's act of taking responsibility.[8]

Argument 2: A Contractualist Defence of Normative Powers

In the previous section, I used the description of answerability interests as part of an Owens-style argument in favour of a normative power of taking responsibility. In this section, I will show that my substantial points about answerability interests can also be part of a contractualist argument.

Contractualists think that correct moral principles are identified by some hypothetical agreement or decision-making. For instance, Scanlon argues that we can identify the correct moral principles by focusing on what 'no one could reasonably reject as a basis for informed, unforced, general agreement' (Scanlon 2000, 153).[9] Normally, such principles concern general requirements and prohibitions. But, as Watson pointed out, they need not be so restricted and can also include principles that confer normative powers on us. In fact, as Watson argued, it seems one could not reasonably reject a principle that endows people with the power of promising:

> The idea is that, in virtue of various interests and values, no one could reasonably reject a principle that conferred the power to bind one's will in this way. … The significance of expectations, coordination, the value of assurance, as well as the interest

[8] At this point, a comparison with Enoch (2012) might be helpful. Enoch discussed the idea of taking responsibility in the context of Williams's famous lorry driver case and argued that one could only take responsibility for what is in the *penumbra* of one's agency, but not for something that is completely unrelated to oneself, such as the movements of the planets. I agree with the basic idea in Enoch's account that taking responsibility requires some form of agential involvement. However, there are also important differences between Enoch's view and mine. In addition to the fact that Enoch does not consider AI-related contexts at all, my view on taking responsibility differs from Enoch's by, firstly, substituting the vague notion of 'penumbra' of agency with a more definite description of 'involvement in the development and use of AI' and, secondly, by using the notion of such involvement to explain who could best satisfy answerability interests, rather than considering it an independent condition.

[9] In this section, I will mainly focus on Scanlon's formulation of contractualism, but my arguments may equally apply to other versions, such as Rawls's contractualism. Rawls does not talk about what no one could reasonably reject, but rather – more positively – what certain parties would *accept* in a situation behind a veil of ignorance. See Rawls (2005).

> in forging mutual commitments, would be registered in the standpoint of reasonable rejection. In this way, promise-making and promise-keeping turn out to answer to deep human needs, just as we understand them to do. (Watson 2009, 164)

But Watson's contractualist rationale not only applies to the normative power of promising. It can also be extended to the power of taking responsibility, as one could not reasonably reject a principle that allows people, under certain circumstances, to take answerability by an act of will. If what I have said in the last section is roughly correct (viz if a normative power of taking responsibility, as described, is needed to satisfy important interests of those who are harmed, as well as the interests of others), then this speaks in favour of a principle allowing such a power to be the basis of our living together, and it speaks against a reasonable rejection of such a principle. Thus, even if one rejects Owens's method of grounding normative powers directly in certain normative interests, one could still accept my substantial points about answerability interests as part of a contractualist defence of the normative power of taking responsibility.

Moreover, it seems that the grounds for a reasonable rejection of the normative power of taking responsibility are already eliminated by the specifications of taking responsibility as presented in the last section. To begin with, one might reasonably reject a focus on liability to blame and punishment, due to the argument given in the section above discussing CT's proposal. Yet, since I focus on answerability, rather than liability, this objection is ruled out. Moreover, one might reasonably reject a principle that allows *anyone* to take responsibility, no matter how remote they are to the harm caused, because such a taking of responsibility would be arbitrary and could be insulting. Yet, with a suitable specification, and in particular a restriction on who is able to satisfy answerability interests, this objection can be ruled out too. Hence, it seems that the specification of taking responsibility, as I understand it, rules out grounds for reasonable rejection and thereby creates contractualist support for the normative power as I described it.[10]

TWO QUESTIONS (AND AN OBJECTION)

Before I conclude, let me address two pressing questions. Why would one ever take responsibility for something bad, given that doing so imposes a burden on

[10] These arguments concern taking responsibility for harmful, as opposed to beneficial, conduct. Therefore, my arguments in favour of taking responsibility will remain restricted to harm. Whether taking responsibility for beneficial action is possible will depend on whether a related normative power could also serve some of our *normative* interests or whether contractualism would adopt a principle that allows taking responsibility for beneficial action. I am doubtful about the prospects of such a view but I will remain neutral on this point for the purposes of this book.

oneself? And relatedly, if taking responsibility remains optional, do we not risk leaving the responsibility gap wide open?

As I outlined earlier in my discussion of Owens, there are virtue-related or relationship-related reasons to take responsibility. By taking responsibility, we can satisfy answerability interests of others and benefit them. Doing so, and thus accepting a burden for ourselves, can be virtuous as well as helping us to create and maintain morally valuable relationships. Thus, insofar as we care about virtue, moral excellence, and our relationships with others, we can have strong reasons to take responsibility in certain circumstances.

This claim should not come as a surprise: the normative power of taking responsibility is similar to the normative power of promising: both concern the imposition of obligations on oneself and the creation of benefits for others; and just as promising is valuable because it assists forming and maintaining relationships with others as well as due to the way it can give others normative control over a situation, taking responsibility can be valuable for similar reasons too. (Understood in this way, this account complements the perspectives of Mason and Wolf discussed in chapter three, who also emphasised relationships and virtue as foundational to the act of taking responsibility.)

In addition, taking responsibility could also be morally obligatory. In chapter three, I discuss the view proposed by Enoch that, at least sometimes, it can be obligatory to exercise a normative power (e.g., to promise, to take responsibility, etc.) even while the normal effect of exercising that power (e.g., promising: obligation; taking responsibility: responsibility) is still absent (see Enoch 2012, 105–106). Even though I argued against linking normative powers too closely to obligations to exercise them – since a lack of discretion can undermine both the value and the very existence of the normative power – I acknowledge the possibility that, at least under some circumstances, exercising a normative power can be obligatory rather than merely optional, and this can also be true of the normative power of taking responsibility. Thus, in principle, there could be deontic (i.e., obligation-related), and not only aretaic (i.e., virtue-related), reasons to take responsibility.

In addition, we can have reason to take responsibility because doing so affirms our practical identity as real-world agents. Wolf explained that there is value in 'expressing our recognition that we are beings who are thoroughly in-the-world, in interaction with others whose movements and thoughts we cannot fully control, and whom we affect and are affected by accidentally as well as intentionally, involuntarily, unwittingly, inescapably, as well as voluntarily and deliberately' (Wolf 2001, 13, 14). But if so, we should not shy away from the harm we faultlessly caused, but rather express, by taking responsibility, that our agency had a morally significant impact, even if such impact and our action alone would not lead to moral responsibility.

But even if these reasons for taking responsibility exist, one might wonder how likely it is that people will *actually* take responsibility and close the responsibility gap. If individuals are free to decide whether to take responsibility, there is indeed no guarantee that someone will actually take responsibility. Thus, whether and how much the responsibility gap will be closed is a contingent fact. It may just be that the responsibility gap becomes a little narrower.

To close responsibility gaps in important areas may therefore require returning to an idea from CT, according to which taking responsibility *ahead of time* is a condition for taking on certain roles or engaging in certain activities. Earlier, I argued that CT's own account could not legitimately demand such prospective responsibility because it would thereby introduce unjustified strict penal liability. However, my own account does not face the same objection, since I focus on responsibility as *answerability* and not on responsibility as *liability*. Thus, in my view, we can make taking responsibility (as answerability) a condition of certain positions, thereby introducing a form of *strict answerability*, without thereby falling prey to the objections against *strict liability*.[11] Hence, there is greater room for regulating taking prospective responsibility in my view and thereby ensuring that responsibility gaps will be closed more effectively. Yet, even here, we cannot completely guarantee that the responsibility gap will be fully closed and we should therefore acknowledge the limited, yet still very important role, that taking responsibility can play. (This reinforces the thought that taking responsibility and strict moral answerability have to be combined as a solution in the context of AI. I shall return to this thought later.)

But there may be a final objection to my view. Earlier, I claimed that the interests of the victims of harm play an important role in supporting the normative power of taking responsibility. However, this argument might go too far for my purposes: the victims' interests alone may be strong enough to create certain obligations, so that a separate act of taking responsibility would no longer be needed for those obligations to arise. If so, the act of taking responsibility would be redundant.

To respond to this objection, let me clarify the interests under consideration. In my earlier argument, I focused on what I called the victims' *answerability* interests. Answerability interests are *normative* interests, ie interests that other people *have an obligation* to do certain things, rather than *factual* interests, ie interests that other people simply *do* these things. However, no matter how strong the *normative* interests of person A are that person B has a certain obligation towards them, such interests alone cannot create that obligation. For instance, no matter how strong my neighbour's normative interest is that I am obliged to paint his house, this interest alone does not create such an obligation for me. Similarly, no matter how strong the victims' normative interest is that someone

[11] To clarify again: strict *answerability* and strict *liability* both apply to someone solely by virtue of his conduct and independent from mental states such as intent, negligence, or recklessness. Yet, strict answerability means that, as a result of such conduct, a person is obliged to answer to others whereas strict liability means that a person can be blamed (in the moral context), or convicted, punished, respectively obliged to pay compensation (in the legal context).

be obliged to explain, apologise and follow up, such interest alone cannot create these obligations. Therefore, taking responsibility is not redundant.

However, there may be a stronger version of this objection once we consider the victims' *factual* interests, ie the victims' interests in *actually receiving* an explanation, apology and follow-up, as opposed to the *normative* interests in *being owed* these things. If victims' factual interests are sufficiently strong, they alone could be reason enough to require satisfaction by whomever is in a position to provide it. Moreover, such reasons could even create an obligation, at least if one accepts the principle that it is obligatory to help others when doing so would greatly benefit them and not impose on them any significant burden (*cf* Singer 1972). Hence, in such cases, an act of taking responsibility could be unnecessary for certain obligations to arise.

For the sake of argument, I will grant that positive obligations can arise from factual interests and I thereby disregard libertarian (or liberal) objections to such a position. But even then, it is doubtful whether factual interests can generate the *right kinds* of obligation. To begin with, positive obligations arising from the interests or needs of others are normally *imperfect* obligations in the sense that they do not correspond to specific claim-rights. But having such claim-rights, and being able to control the corresponding obligations, is exactly what the victims have a normative interest in, or so I have argued.

Moreover, factual interests cannot generate the obligation to apologise, because giving a genuine and fitting apology for something requires that one is also responsible for it, and not just that apologising would have positive consequences. As Govier and Verwoerd explain, 'to apologize for an action is to admit that … one was responsible for it' (Govier and Verwoerd 2002, 69) and Shuman adds: 'to be meaningful, an apology must … acknowledge responsibility' (Shuman 2000, 185; see also Gill 2000; S Harris, Grainger and Mullany 2006; N Smith 2008; Cunningham 2014;). Thus, without responsibility, what is meant to be an apology just ends up as an expression of regret or disappointment. The prospect of satisfying certain interests alone cannot make an apology any more appropriate, let alone obligatory, than the prospect of satisfying certain interests can make punishing someone appropriate.

However, even if we set aside these points too and assume that factual interests can generate the right obligations (ie *perfect* obligations and an obligation to apologise), the act of taking responsibility would still not be redundant. A comparison to promising, which also concerns imposing obligations on oneself, can show why.

Suppose my friend really needs my help to move house and he also helped me in the past. My friend's strong factual interest in my help, together with the norms of friendship, make it obligatory for me to help him. Thus, no further promise is needed to create this obligation for me. However, even if I subsequently *also* promise to help him, this promise is still significant. To begin with, my promise can still specify an otherwise vaguer obligation, potentially increase its stringency, and make it an explicit part of our interaction. But most importantly, the fact that there are *some* cases where interests alone create an obligation does not imply that this is always so. In fact, in most cases, my friend's interests do not create an obligation for me, so that my power of promising and creating an obligation at will still retains its full value in these cases.

What is true of promises in these regards is also true of taking responsibility. Even when the victims' factual interests create obligations on their own, taking responsibility can still add value. In taking responsibility, a person can specify an otherwise vague obligation, increase the stringency of an obligation, and make it an explicit part of a future interaction. What is more, in the context of AI, there are often numerous people who could satisfy the victims' interests so that the act of taking responsibility could also provide victims with a specific addressee whom they would otherwise lack. But most importantly, and just as in the case of promising, the fact that there are *some* cases where interests alone create certain obligations does not imply that this is always so. In fact, in most cases the victims' interests will not create obligations, which means that the power of taking responsibility will retain its full value in these cases.

Thus, even if we concede that factual interests alone can generate the right kinds of obligation (which I argued is not the case), the normative power of taking responsibility is still not redundant and retains its value.

CONCLUSION

In this chapter, I accepted – for the sake of argument – that certain AI systems cause responsibility gaps, and I asked whether we could close those gaps *at will*, viz by exercising a normative power of taking responsibility. I first rejected CT's view of *taking prospective liability*, a view according to which a military commander can, ahead of time, accept liability to blame and punishment for any harm caused by autonomous weapon systems under her command. Instead, I defended a view of *taking retrospective answerability*, viz the view that people can make themselves morally answerable for the harm caused by AI systems, not only ahead of time, but also when harm has already been caused.

My view shows that a normative power of taking responsibility can close AI's responsibility gap, but only within certain limitations. Since I specifically focus on answerability, my view can close an *answerability* gap, but not necessarily a *liability* gap. Yet, ensuring answerability is an important step in addressing the responsibility gap and, what is more, the normative power I defended can close this answerability gap more effectively than CT's proposal could ever close a liability gap. Since I focus on answerability (as opposed to the much more burdensome liability), taking such answerability can be made more easily a condition of accepting certain roles. After all, when being held answerable, a person would be addressed as a rational moral agent, deserving of a genuine moral conversation, and not – as in cases of being held strictly liable – be a mere passive object of blame or punishment. In addition, I also introduced the possibility of taking *retrospective* responsibility, in addition to *prospective* responsibility, thereby providing another route to closing the responsibility gap. Furthermore, given the reasons people have to exercise the normative power of taking responsibility as answerability, it is more likely that people will actually make themselves answerable than it is that they will make themselves liable to blame and punishment.

Finally, I have based my arguments on the assumption that responsibility gaps exist, so that 'taking' responsibility would amount to 'creating' responsibility when there would otherwise be none. However, my approach could also remain attractive to those who deny responsibility gaps. These scholars could think of taking responsibility, not as a way of 'creating' responsibility, but rather as a way of 'transferring' responsibility from, say, a group of people where it is highly unclear whether anyone has more than a marginal share of responsibility, to someone who will then take on that responsibility as the primary holder. Taking responsibility in this sense could also satisfy important answerability interests of others and lead to a contractualist principle that one could not reasonably reject. Hence, taking responsibility as a normative power, understood in the sense of 'transferring' responsibility, could be supported even in the absence of responsibility gaps.

9

AI and the Value of Responsibility

CURRENT SCHOLARSHIP IN AI ethics has provided important resources in analysing various challenges around responsibility. However, in so doing, it has focused predominantly on the potential *absence* of moral responsibility and has given short shrift to what exactly the *need* for, or *value* of, moral responsibility is. This is unfortunate since the concern around responsibility gaps is a combination of both aspects: it comprises not only the *absence* of responsibility for AI-induced harm, but it also implies the *need* for responsibility. After all, if there is no need for (human) responsibility, as in the case of the movements of the planets, we do not talk about a responsibility gap in the first place. As a result, there are also two ways of denying a responsibility gap: either by denying the *absence* of responsibility or by denying the *need* for responsibility.

Moreover, the need for, or value of, moral responsibility also receives special significance in the context of AI, as compared with my discussion of responsibility in Part I of this book. This is because the lorry driver case concerned one specific scenario and I have so far discussed responsibility primarily as a condition of a genuine apology. In the context of AI, however, questions about responsibility receive a more systemic dimension, since the prevalent use of AI transcends the individual lorry driver cases and could have much wider implications beyond the aptitude of apologies.

I shall therefore focus on the value of moral responsibility in this chapter, responding to those who deny such value in the context of AI and who could, therefore, also be understood as denying responsibility gaps in this way. If their perspective is correct, then the previously discussed solutions regarding strict answerability and taking responsibility are not necessary, and we could consider insurance schemes without responsibility instead. In other words, the significance of the previous ideas about responsibility requires clarification that responsibility is truly significant in the context of AI. To investigate this issue, I shall address prominent views that deny or relativise the value of responsibility. Although I build on some of their insights, I shall also argue that the absence of responsibility would be problematic, both on practical grounds, as it leads to undesirable consequences, and on theoretical grounds, as it is ultimately even an inconsistent proposition. The conclusion of this chapter is that responsibility is important; the *Autonomous AI Conundrum* is reinforced, and we need to rethink our current frameworks of responsibility.

THE VALUE OF LACKING RESPONSIBILITY FOR AI

The strongest case against the value of responsibility comes in two parts: one is negative, aiming to debunk existing strategies supporting the value of responsibility; and the other is positive, advocating for the value of a lack of responsibility.

Peter Königs presents the negative part by arguing that 'responsibility gaps, assuming they exist, are just not that problematic' (Königs 2022, 2). He specifically counters two concerns about the absence of responsibility. The first is that it might 'incentivize harmful behavior' (Königs 2022, 2). This perspective is held by Deborah Johnson, who suggests that assigning responsibility will 'keep the pressure on developers to ensure the safety and reliability of such devices' (Johnson 2015, 714). Similarly, Filippo Santoni de Sio and Giulio Mecacci observe that 'the more persons designing, regulating, and operating the system can legitimately (and possibly systematically) avoid blame for their wrong behaviour, the less these agents will be incentivised to prevent these wrong behaviours' (Santoni de Sio and Mecacci 2021, 1063).

However, Königs objects. The idea that individuals can exploit the shadow of 'responsibility gaps' and engage in careless or even deliberately harmful actions without facing consequences is fundamentally flawed, Königs argues (Königs 2022, 5). In situations where there is negligence or fault, such as with a manufacturer, programmer or operator whose actions lead to an autonomous system causing harm, it is entirely appropriate and necessary to assign responsibility to that individual or group of individuals. Thus, Königs adds, '[i]f responsibility gaps arise at all, they do not arise in situations in which people act without due care' (Königs 2022, 5). Instead, these gaps are pertinent in unique cases where harm occurs without detectable fault or negligence, ie situations where people could not sensibly have any further incentive to behave carefully. Therefore, Königs concludes, the absence of responsibility in cases of harm without fault does not, in fact, encourage careless behaviour. Even in the presence of responsibility gaps, there remains a strong incentive for individuals to adhere to a certain standard of care. This standard, which can vary in its level of strictness (and, in fact, be very high in some contexts), serves as a crucial guideline for behaviour. I believe that Königs is correct in his critique, and that responsibility gaps would not incentivise careless conduct.

Königs then moves on to a second worry, which mainly draws on the use of AI in military contexts and which holds that responsibility gaps constitute disrespect. Sparrow, who holds such a view, puts it as follows:

> It is a minimal expression of respect due to our enemy – if war is going to be governed by morality at all – that someone should accept responsibility, or be capable of being held responsible, for the decision to take their life. If we fail in this, we treat our enemy like vermin, as though they may be exterminated without moral regard at all. The least we owe our enemies is allowing that their lives are of sufficient worth that someone should accept responsibility for their deaths. (Sparrow 2007, 67)

Thus, Sparrow highlights the ethical obligation in war to accept responsibility for taking an enemy's life, asserting that failing to do so diminishes their humanity, or even dehumanises them as objects or animals. But Königs opposes this view:

> Weighing goods is notoriously difficult, but if we had to choose between sending a message of respect by renouncing autonomous weapons and, say, saving the life of a single human being, soldier or civilian, the choice should be obvious. The importance of signaling respect pales in comparison to that of the other goods at stake in war. (Königs 2022, 8)

Königs underscores the complexity of different factors that must be considered, particularly in the context of warfare. He recognises the value of expressing respect, but he posits that in war there are more significant considerations, such as the protection of lives, which could potentially outweigh the need to express respect. This perspective invites us to evaluate which of these elements carries greater weight.

It is important to note that Königs does not dismiss the relevance of respect-related concerns about responsibility altogether; rather, he suggests that they might be superseded by other factors. The concept of pro-tanto reasons can help us to clarify this position. Even if Königs is right that there are other more important considerations, there are still also pro-tanto reasons to ensure responsibility, ie reasons with a certain weight, which continue to be valid despite the presence of other considerations. It just so happens that the other considerations override the pro-tanto reasons for expressing respect and responsibility. As a result, a certain need for responsibility persists, and this differentiates Königs' response to this second worry from his response to the first. While Königs fully rejected the first worry, by arguing that responsibility gaps do not incentivise careless conduct at all, he only relativises the second worry by claiming that the valid reasons to try to ensure responsibility and respect could sometimes be superseded by other, more important considerations. Consequently, the implication is that we must undertake a case-by-case analysis, weighing the merits of responsibility and respect against other significant aspects.

I conclude that Königs makes a plausible case that two of the most prominent strategies to argue for the value of responsibility are subject to powerful criticisms, leaving unclear why or to what extent we should aim to prevent responsibility gaps from occurring. In what follows, I shall now go beyond Königs' opposition to existing rationales and consider an even more radical position, presented by John Danaher, and according to which responsibility gaps are not only 'not that problematic', as Königs put it, but 'should [even] be welcomed' (Danaher 2022, 2).

Danaher thinks that at least a subset of responsibility gaps can have positive value for us, especially when they arise in the context of so-called 'tragic choices'. Choices are 'tragic' when 'they involve irresolvable conflicts between different moral considerations and any attempted resolution of such conflicts necessarily leaves a moral "taint" or remainder' (Danaher 2022, 6). In such cases, it is impossible to make a morally flawless decision. Whatever one does, one flouts some norm or other.

Danaher considers three different responses to tragic choices. First, there is what he calls *illusionism*, which is, in Danaher's view, the erroneous denial that there can be genuinely tragic choices. This stance would argue that we should 'convince ourselves that our choices are not tragic or that our decisions leave no moral remainders' (Danaher 2022, 10). Danaher claims that this view fails as it cannot account for what he sees as an undeniable dimension of our moral reality, namely that sometimes such tragic choices inevitably exist. Yet, Danaher also concedes that this strategy might be advantageous in maintaining a certain sense of optimism and reducing psychological stress.

Second, there is the strategy of what Danaher calls *responsibilisation*, which means that 'we confront the tragic choice head-on and accept responsibility for resolving the conflict in a particular way. … We embrace the fact that life sometimes involves these tragic tradeoffs and we live with the consequences' (Danaher 2022, 14). Danaher says that responsibilisation might help us develop our moral agency and even certain virtues when dealing with adversities and decisional complexity. But Danaher also highlights disadvantages and claims that 'responsibilisation has a dark side' (Danaher 2022, 14), most notably due to its tendency to encourage us to 'blame too quickly, ignore mitigating factors, impose harsh punishment and draw unjustified conclusions about the capacity of people to control their choices' (Danaher 2022, 14). As a result, people 'are often made to suffer unjustly, both psychologically and physically, through practices of blame and punishment' (Danaher 2022, 14). Moreover, in cases of tragic choices, simply holding people responsible, Danaher adds, 'is all too often an invitation to ignore the tragedy involved in those choices and to punish people unfairly for not following our moral intuitions' (Danaher 2022, 15).

Finally, there is a third way of responding to tragic choices, namely *delegation*, which is 'where we get someone (or some thing) to make tragic choices on our behalf. We shift the burden of resolving the conflict away from ourselves' (Danaher 2022, 12). Danaher finds difficulties here too. For a start, it could diminish our moral skills: 'If we delegate too readily, our moral "muscles" may atrophy. We may never do the hard work of trying to figure out what is right or wrong for ourselves' (Danaher 2022, 14). Moreover, delegating tasks and burdens does not mean eliminating them: 'In fact, it may just concentrate the burden on particular individuals who suffer more greatly as a result' (Danaher 2022, 13). On the other hand, Danaher adds, 'delegation is psychologically attractive' (Danaher 2022, 13), at least for those who can offload their tasks and burdens, as 'it shifts the psychological and moral costs of the tragic choice away from them' (Danaher 2022, 12).

In summary, we have the following options (Danaher 2022, 15): Illusionism offers the benefit of 'reducing psychological stress' and 'help[ing] to maintain sense of optimism and moral rectitude'. However, it comes at the cost of 'reward[ing] ignorance and avoidance of truth' and is ultimately 'unstable and fragile'. Responsibilisation 'develops moral agency and virtue, accepts reality of tragedy and embraces compromise'. On the downside, it risks the 'danger of scapegoating', the problem of 'assuming more responsibility than we rightfully deserve to bear', and the 'psychological and physical distress of excess blame and punishment'. And delegation allows for the 'shift[ing] [of] psychological and moral burden onto an entity that is better able to bear that burden', thereby also 'reduc[ing] psychological stress'. But its costs include the 'corrosion or atrophy of moral agency' and an 'excessive concentration of stress and moral burden on particular individuals and institutions'.

Danaher states clearly that 'none of these solutions is ideal. Each has its benefits and costs' (Danaher 2022, 15), and we may need to determine the attractiveness of each option on a case-by-case basis. But Danaher makes an interesting observation. In the context of new technologies, especially high-performing AI, the strategy of delegation might become more attractive. He says:

> The advantage of delegation to machines is that it gives us the benefits of ordinary delegation without the typical associated costs. Machines do not have to suffer the psychological and moral distress of human agents. They can resolve conflicts without bearing the burden. (Danaher 2022, 16)

Thus, delegating tasks to machines enables us to enjoy the benefits of offloading tasks without transferring stress to another sentient being. Moreover, since a 'decision to delegate can be fully justified and blameless in a way that a decision to resolve a tragic choice may not be; and vice versa' (Danaher 2022, 19), we may finally be able to avoid situations where there is no justified and blameless way out. Danaher even argues that autonomous machines could be a positive disruptive force of our social practices, namely a force that separates tragic choices from the unjust expectation that someone should take responsibility for them or even be blamed or punished (*cf* Danaher 2022, 20). However, such benefits and disruption are only available 'if we accept that it [ie delegation] will result in a type of responsibility gap; the machine cannot be responsible, nor is it appropriate or desirable to trace responsibility to us' (Danaher 2022, 16).

Danaher's view is insightful. It shows how we can potentially reframe responsibility gaps as a form of beneficial, cost-reduced delegation. Moreover, it is noteworthy that Danaher's claims about responsibility can apply to a broad spectrum of responsibility types. Danaher's framework explicitly addresses both prospective (forward-looking) and retrospective (backward-looking) aspects of responsibility. Prospective responsibility, involving the obligation to make certain decisions, can lead to psychological strain due to the associated decision-making burdens. Retrospective responsibility, on the other hand, can include emotional repercussions, such as guilt and remorse, and also constitute a psychological burden (*cf* Danaher 2022, 6, 16). Furthermore, Danaher's view can take into account yet another dimension of responsibility, even though he does not make this explicit. It can cover not only responsibility as blameworthiness but also responsibility as answerability. The psychological discomfort arising from self-blame or blame from others is widely recognised. Yet, the obligation to justify one's actions, as part of one's answerability, also presents its own psychological burdens and costs. Individuals may find it strenuous to defend their decisions, even when these decisions are entirely rational.

At this point, a brief digression to David Velleman's work can help. Although Velleman focused on an alleged right to euthanasia, and thus on a very different topic, some of his arguments against such a right hold significance for my present purposes too. Velleman claimed that '[o]ptions can be undesirable … because they subject one to various kinds of pressure' (Velleman 2015, 10), most notably psychological or social pressure, even if the decision turns out to be perfectly rational. This clearly resonates with Danaher's 'tragic' choices. Moreover, options can be undesirable or even harmful when they remove a particular state of affairs as the 'unchosen' status quo, and create a situation in which any outcome becomes intimately linked to a person due to their choosing it: 'Having choices can thus deprive one of desirable outcomes whose desirability depends on their being unchosen' (Velleman 2015, 11). And once people can make a choice, they become answerable, which can also be a burden. In Velleman's words:

> [I]f others regard you as choosing a state of affairs, they will hold you responsible for it; and if they hold you responsible for a state of affairs, they can ask you to justify it. (Velleman 2015, 12)
>
> [P]eople care, and are right to care, about whether they can justify their choices to others. Of course, this concern can easily seem like slavishness or neurotic insecurity; but it should not be dismissed too lightly. Our ability to justify our choices to the people around us is what enables us to sustain the role of rational agent in our dealings with them; and it is therefore essential to our remaining, in their eyes, eligible partners in cooperation and conversation, or appropriate objects of respect. (Velleman 2015, 13)

These points hold for tragic choices too. When people have to make a choice about which morally flawed option to pick, they will experience the psychological pressure associated with it. They are deprived of a situation where they could otherwise dissociate themselves from the morally flawed outcome since, in this instance, the option was chosen *by them*, and they therefore face the burden of having to justify, or perceiving themselves under an obligation to justify, their decision to others. On this basis, then, a form of (perceived) answerability for tragic choices can burden or even harm people, even when they are perfect decision-makers and even if blame is off the table. I therefore conclude that the strongest version of Danaher's view can include various types of responsibility, including responsibility in terms of liability to blame, but also to responsibility in terms of answerability.

Before I go on to critique Danaher's view, I wish to suggest two additional modifications, which I think could strengthen his account even further. The first modification concerns the explanation of the unfavourable aspects of responsibility. Danaher predominantly underscores the psychological burdens of being responsible, such as the pressure or guilt accompanying responsibility. However, he could have done more to include other aspects too. Responsibility for transgressions can be inherently adverse or harmful for someone, irrespective of one's psychological disposition or experience. For instance, Victor Tadros contends that 'it is disvaluable for a person to be responsible for wrongdoing both for instrumental reasons and as such' (Tadros 2020b, 6). Instrumental reasons concern the afflictive consequences of being responsible, such as the burden of being answerable to others, the sting of blame, and the detriments of sanctions. But, in addition, being responsible for wrongdoing can also be disvaluable 'as such', ie 'it is disvaluable for a person's sake that she is responsible for wrongdoing as such, independently of the actual or likely consequences of being responsible, or what it makes apt' (Tadros 2020b, 9). When one acts wrongly, Tadros says, one fails to respond appropriately to (at least some of) the moral reasons there are. And if this happens, Tadros adds, a person's 'life is less good' (Tadros 2020b, 12) in the sense that 'she therefore has less reason to value the fact that her life is lived in that way' (Tadros 2020b, 12). To illustrate this view, Tadros uses the following example:

> Suppose that you wake up from a coma, knowing that you have been involved in a serious assault, but not knowing whether you committed the assault or were the victim of it. As long as the consequences are not awful, I would much prefer to be the victim of the assault. The vast majority of those I have asked share this view. (Tadros 2020b, 10)

Although Tadros's view concerns culpable wrongdoing in non-dilemmatic situations, his arguments can (at least partly) apply to the context of tragic choices too. Acting wrongly, even if this was inevitable, makes a person's life worse in the sense Tadros describes: that person has 'less reason to value the fact that her life is lived in that way' (Tadros 2020b, 12).

A more expansive interpretation of Danaher's stance would amalgamate these elements, acknowledging that responsibility can be deleterious due to psychological strains, adverse outcomes like blame or sanctions, and intrinsic negativity.[1]

[1] See also Munch, Mainz and Bjerring (2023), who also apply Tadros's view to the context of AI.

The second modification concerns the focus on 'tragic' choices. On a strong reading, which Danaher seems to suggest, tragic choices concern 'irresolvable conflicts between different moral considerations' (Danaher 2022, 6) such that whatever one does, one acts wrongly. It is this understanding that Nagel also discussed when he asked whether the world could not only be a 'bad' place but also an 'evil' place by placing humans in situations where they can only act wrongly (Nagel 1979, chapter 'War and Massacre'). As Danaher himself points out, the existence of such situations has remained controversial, and often opposed, for instance along the following lines. Morally, one always ought to choose the correct action. Moreover, the principle 'ought implies can' suggests that if one ought to do something, then it must be possible to do it. Consequently, it is impossible for a situation to exist where one is morally obligated to act, but cannot act correctly. In other words, it is impossible for all available options to be morally wrong.

In response, I recommend that Danaher not challenge this argument in detail, but rather offer a less controversial reading of 'tragic' choices. A weaker version of tragic choices would hold that each choice allows for a full justification, but concerns a situation where important goods or values are outweighed or silenced by more important considerations, such that it becomes fitting to feel agent-regret in Williams's sense. So understood, Danaher can retain the focus on tragic choices as an important part of this argument while sidestepping too controversial an issue for his purposes.

THE VALUES OF MORAL RESPONSIBILITY

Danaher's account shows one limitation and two biases. The limitation is the constrained focus on tragic choices. So even if we follow Danaher completely, we still cannot rule out the problematic nature of responsibility gaps altogether. We may only find them less problematic, or valuable, in the subset of cases that can be aptly described as 'tragic'. However, even there, two biases arise. There is a negativity bias in the sense that Danaher mainly draws on the disadvantages of responsibility without giving sufficient attention to the advantages of responsibility, as explored in the philosophical literature. Furthermore, there is an agent bias in the sense that the account only focuses on the agent of responsibility, ie the bearer of responsibility, and neglects the patient of responsibility, ie those to whom responsibility is owed. After all, as Duff and Coeckelbergh point out, responsibility is a three-part relation: (i) someone (agent) is responsible (ii) for something (object) (iii) to someone (patient) (Duff 2009a; Coeckelbergh 2020). Thus, whenever we consider the value of responsibility, we need to consider the perspectives of both agents and patients. In what follows, I shall explore ways to overcome the two biases, starting with the latter.

Patients of Responsibility

Even if – and this remains to be seen – bearing responsibility is in some way bad, burdensome, or disadvantageous for the agents of responsibility, this does not imply that it is not crucial for the patients of responsibility. In fact, when people suffer harm, especially from the use of technology that was deliberately developed and put into use, they may have an important interest that such harm does not go unaccounted for, or without human responsibility attached. The patients of responsibility may justifiably demand an explanation of what happened, including in terms of the rights and obligations that were at stake, as well as the identification of agents of responsibility they could hold to account. In an earlier publication, and repeated in chapter eight of this book, I have built on the work of Owens and made the following remark:

> When we suffer harm through other people's action, we have an interest that some people not only plan to or de facto explain to us what happened, follow up on us, etc., but also that they morally owe this to us. The existence of such moral obligations is important because, when other people have these obligations, this signifies that our having been harmed is not just some natural misfortune or a case of a damaged object, i.e. something to be filed in an insurance company's drawer, but rather something that requires interpersonal moral acknowledgment. Moreover, it is important to us that we can also control those moral obligations of others by deciding whether or not to release them from these obligations, just as it is important for us to control others' obligations in this way in the context of promising. (Kiener 2022, 584)

Thus, creating a responsibility gap through Danaher's cost-reduced delegation may be beneficial for the agent of responsibility, but it risks frustrating the important interests of the patients of responsibility. And if my previous argument is correct, these are important and morally justified interests that need to be considered. On a consequentialist assessment, it seems entirely possible that these patient interests in avoiding responsibility might be greater in number and weight than the interests of the agents of responsibility in a situation of cost-reduced delegation. Moreover, on a contractualist assessment, it seems possible that the patients of responsibility have a greater complaint against principles that allow the creation of responsibility gaps than the agents of responsibility have when such principles are rejected. Both rationales would require further investigation. But at this point, I only wish to state that there are important considerations that Danaher has not considered, and which further relativise his conclusion that responsibility gaps ought to be welcomed. The best way to understand this claim is that these gaps may be welcomed *by some, but not others*, and that, therefore, there may be *pro-tanto, but certainly not decisive* reasons in favour of them.

Overcoming the Negativity Bias

My second concern is a negativity bias, ie the overemphasis on the negative and burdensome aspects of responsibility without paying sufficient attention to the positive sides, even from the perspective of the agents of responsibility. It is here that the philosophical literature outside AI ethics could provide an important resource. Scholars have pointed to various valuable aspects of responsibility, which we can cluster around three themes.[2]

Responsibility and Morality

First, responsibility supports morality. In what follows, I shall pick out some prominent accounts in this respect. Although these accounts primarily focus on the value of reactive attitudes and blame, they also hold insights about moral responsibility more generally. A first notable account comes from Victoria McGeer, who underscores the dual nature of reactive attitudes (eg resentment, indignation) in moral and social contexts. She claims that our practices and attitudes towards holding each other responsible are not just retrospective judgements. Instead, they also possess a 'proleptic' character – that is, they actively contribute to fostering and maintaining our ability to discern and act upon moral reasons. Expanding on this, McGeer argues that these attitudes are, therefore, equally forward-looking, or what she calls 'evocative'. In her words, reactive attitudes

> are not in their nature merely backward-looking 'reactive' attitudes; they are also forward-looking 'evocative' attitudes, as we might say (McGeer & Pettit, 2015), calling for a particular response from the putative wrongdoer: for instance, to explain and/or justify what they have done; and where that fails, to acknowledge how they have failed to track and respond to the reasons that ought to govern their behaviour, and to commit to doing better in the future. (McGeer 2019, 314)

Note that McGeer's view features not only reactive attitudes like blame but also a form of answerability. Moreover, McGeer emphasises the importance of these attitudes and practices of answerability in 'developing and sustaining our capacity for (socially negotiated) moral-reasons-responsiveness' (McGeer 2019, 314). This implies that such attitudes are not just personal but are embedded within a social framework where moral reasoning and responsibility are negotiated and upheld. They are, therefore, integral to the scaffolding that underpins what it means to be a morally responsible agent.

[2] Note that there is an important and subtle difference between this section and the Owens-style argument outlined earlier. This section focuses on the value of responsibility as such while the Owens-style argument (and also my discussion of taking responsibility) focused on the value of the *normative power* to take responsibility.

Another important account comes from Fricker, who offers a view on the value of blame, according to which blame is a practice fundamentally designed to promote a better alignment between the moral understandings of the blamer and the blamed. Fricker holds that the primary aim of blame is to expand the moral awareness of the person who has done wrong. This expansion of awareness is not an isolated goal. Rather, it is intrinsically linked to the shaping of the reasons that guide our behaviour. So understood, blame is seen as a communicative tool that not only aligns moral understandings but also aligns the moral reasons that motivate individuals. She asserts that this paradigm of blame is not a manifestation of negative sentiments but rather a means of encouraging the wrongdoer to adopt the perspective of the wronged party. This process is intended to broaden their perception and modify their motivations. In Fricker's words:

> The picture of blame that has now emerged is of a practice that is fundamentally aimed at promoting greater alignment between the moral understandings of the blamer and the blamee by enlarging the moral awareness of the wrongdoer. But next we must acknowledge that this is not a stand-alone purpose, for our moral understandings affect the reasons that govern our behaviour. Closely related, then, is the increased alignment of the moral reasons that motivate us. (Fricker 2016, 175)

Comparing Fricker's view with McGeer's, we find that both scholars emphasise the forward-looking and developmental aspects of moral practices – blame in Fricker's case and responsibility practices more generally in McGeer's. While McGeer focuses on the 'proleptic' nature of holding responsible – how it helps to develop and sustain our capacity for moral reasoning and action, Fricker highlights blame as a communicative process aimed at aligning moral understandings and reasons between individuals. But both views depart from traditional notions that see these practices as solely retrospective judgements. Instead, they underscore a dynamic interaction: McGeer views responsibility as a cultivation tool for moral agency, and Fricker sees blame as a communicative act to bridge moral perceptions and motivations. Both perspectives highlight the transformative potential of these practices in moral development and understanding, suggesting a nuanced, interactive approach to moral reasoning and behaviour.

Finally, Shoemaker and Manuel Vargas offer a perspective on blame that focuses on its role as a communicative function, emphasising the expression and reinforcement of normative commitments. According to their view, 'blame's core unifying feature, namely, its *function*, … is to signal the blamer's commitment to a set of norms' (Shoemaker and Vargas 2021, 581, original emphasis). Thus, when someone blames another, they are not merely pointing out some wrongdoing; they are communicating important information about their own values and expectations. This act of blaming conveys that the norms breached by the blamed party are significant to the blamer, and that such violations are not to be overlooked. Furthermore, this communication can be seen as an invitation for the blamed party to reaffirm their commitment to these norms. Shoemaker and Vargas also highlight that, by enforcing norms, the blamer is signalling their identity as part of a 'moral tribe'. They are declaring what they stand for, the practical reasons they uphold, and their disposition towards upholding these norms. This aspect encompasses broader implications about how they view themselves as practical agents, including expectations about how they should be treated by others.

The common ground among McGeer, Fricker, and Shoemaker and Vargas lies in their view that responsibility and blame are not merely retrospective judgments but proactive, communicative practices that shape moral understanding and behaviour within social contexts. The key difference is their focus: McGeer emphasises the developmental role of responsibility in fostering moral agency; Fricker highlights blame's role in aligning moral understandings and motivations; and Shoemaker and Vargas concentrate on blame as a signal of normative commitments and identity within a moral community.

However, it is noteworthy that the perspectives of McGeer, Fricker, and Shoemaker and Vargas on the value of blame can be extended to the concept of answerability, independent of blame. Like blame, answerability serves as a proactive, communicative mechanism that fosters moral understanding and reinforces social norms and expectations. It involves a process of holding oneself and others accountable to moral standards, thereby contributing to the development of moral agency and the alignment of moral values within a community, echoing the themes emphasised by these authors in the context of blame.

The extension to answerability is also particularly important for another reason. The value of blame, as elucidated by McGeer, Fricker, and Shoemaker and Vargas, hinges on the premise that the individual being blamed is also *worthy* of blame, implying a sense of fault or culpability. Their perspectives collectively suggest that blame's constructive role in shaping moral understanding, aligning moral reasons, and signalling normative commitments relies on the assumption that the blamee has committed a culpable violation or wrongdoing. If there is no fault or culpability, the intended value and effectiveness of blaming, as described by these authors, would not arise, as the foundational rationale for blame – that of addressing a genuine moral transgression and prompting a meaningful response – would be absent.

The value of answerability, in contrast to blame, is not contingent upon fault or culpability. Answerability as a concept emphasises the responsibility of individuals to account for their actions and decisions within a moral or social framework, irrespective of whether those actions are blameworthy. As such, answerability focuses on the ongoing duty to explain and justify one's conduct, fostering transparency and moral reflection, which are valuable regardless of the presence of fault or culpability. This is particularly significant in contexts where the concept of responsibility without fault is a key consideration. And indeed, the context of AI and potential responsibility gaps presents a scenario where traditional notions of fault may not apply, making these views particularly relevant. In the realm of AI, where assigning blame can be complex due to the lack of conventional fault or culpability, the insights of McGeer, Fricker, and Shoemaker and Vargas need to be extended to answerability, since they can then offer a significant perspective on the value of responsibility.

Responsibility and Relationships

Moving on from the claim that responsibility supports morality, I shall now focus on a second strand in the literature, which has scholars arguing that responsibility is valuable because it is constitutive of certain relationships, eg friendship, parenthood, or the patient-physician relationship (Wallace 1994; Owens 2012; Mason 2019). Owens and Mason claimed that even if responsibility, including blame, has a sting in the moment, it is nevertheless an important part of maintaining relationships. Since responsibility is essentially relational too, ie someone is responsible to someone, not holding each other responsible can also lead to estrangement.

Owens explores the nuanced role of blame and guilt in friendships. He argues that even if neither blame nor guilt are intrinsically valuable, their appropriateness in certain situations, particularly within friendships, is beneficial. Owens suggests that valuable relationships often involve obligations, and the habitual practice of blaming one another for breaches of these obligations is essential for maintaining these bonds. This habit of blame is therefore seen as positive for the enrichment it brings to relationships. In his words:

> [B]lame (and guilt) can be a positive feature of our lives. For one thing, certain valuable relationships involve obligation and breach of an obligation often renders one vulnerable to blame. These obligation-involving relationships exist only where people are in the habit of blaming certain kinds of action. Since our lives are enriched once we enjoy these relations with others, the habits of blame that help to constitute such bonds are good for us. Our interest in these habits of blame is one aspect of our interest in enjoying those relationships. (Owens 2012, 25)

Mason focuses on the concept of what she calls 'extended responsibility' in personal relationships, emphasising that this extension is aimed at respecting others and securing their trust. This responsibility goes beyond mere liability and is necessary for participating in the moral community, rather than constituting a moral obligation. Relationships entail various duties, both practical and emotional, such as nurturing, protection and loyalty. The interpretation of these duties varies across relationships. In personal relationships especially, like friendship, a special form of mutual accountability and obligations is essential for this relationship. Mason says:

> Think of a romantic relationship in which one person gradually stops seeing their partner as a proper interlocutor, stops holding them accountable. That is a sign that the relationship has dissolved. Although being blameworthy, and being blamed, sting in the moment, over the long term it is the better way to be. Taking responsibility is part of being in relationships, part of being a member of a community. We can let

> go of all that, but estrangement and alienation are a high price to pay for avoiding blameworthiness. (Mason 2019, 201)

Mason views blame as a communicative tool within relationships, serving as a means for acknowledging and responding to wrongs done. By accepting responsibility, people show respect and investment in the relationship. Accepting responsibility and expressing remorse are therefore important for maintaining the integrity of personal bonds.

Mason also considers more formal relations, such as the patient-physician relationship, and acknowledges the difficulty in distinguishing when extended responsibility is appropriate as the line between personal and formal relationships is not always clear. Ultimately, she asserts that taking on extended responsibility is context-dependent and varies based on the relationship's worth and the social context. But it is not too far-fetched to think that relationships such as patient-physician, state-citizen and customer-company are at least partly constituted by certain forms of accountability as well. Thus, if responsibility is absent, these relations will be diminished, and people risk estrangement.

In summary, then, Owens and Mason focus on relationships. While Owens describes how blame can be constitutive of certain relationships, Mason highlights blame as a communicative tool for demonstrating commitment, and these insights can carry over to responsibility as answerability as well. How we hold each other answerable also constitutes important part of our relationships and reflects our commitment to them. Thus if the use of AI were to remove practices of responsibility, it may also impoverish the value of relationships.

Responsibility and Agential Identity

Finally, a third aspect of the value of responsibility, in addition to its value for morality and social relations, is that responsibility is important for our sense as agents in the world. In 'Being in the World', Joseph Raz draws a close connection between responsibility and our self-conception. He says:

> [T]o understand responsibility we need to understand our attachment to consequences of our actions which are beyond our control. The key … lies in the way our actions are related to our sense of who we are. (Raz 2011, 237)

Raz holds this view because he thinks that our understanding of ourselves is largely defined by an acknowledgement of our skills and their boundaries, which he refers to as our 'domains of secure competence'. These domains are areas in our lives where we feel a sense of capability and control. They are integral to how we perceive ourselves and they form a critical part of our identity. As he puts it:

> [C]entral to our way of Being in the World is a permanently evolving sense of our own mastery and its limitations. Our sense of ourselves includes awareness of a domain within which we are confident that, barring competence-defeating events (a seizure, a biased teacher, etc.), if we set ourselves to do something we will. I call it the domain of secure competence. (Raz 2011, 244–245)

Raz suggests that being true to ourselves involves accepting responsibility for the consequences that arise from our actions within these domains, even when these consequences are unforeseeable or beyond our control. This responsibility is not just about accountability for direct actions, but also encompasses the indirect outcomes that flow from these actions. In essence, accepting responsibility in this context is more than a mere acknowledgment of causality; it is about maintaining an honest and coherent self-image. This concept of responsibility is deeply connected to our sense of autonomy and agency. It implies that our self-conception is not static but evolves as we continually engage with, and reflect on, our actions and their impacts, both intended and unintended. Again, in Raz's words:

> In holding ourselves competent within that domain we hold ourselves responsible for actions that fall within it. To disavow responsibility for such actions is to be false to who we are. (Raz 2011, 245)
>
> I am both drawing attention to the practice of holding ourselves responsible for actions within our respective spheres of secure competence and justifying it, by pointing to its role in maintaining our sense of who we are, and of our relations to the world. (Raz 2011, 245)

Thus, in Raz's view, our self-conception is shaped by both our recognition of our competences and our willingness to accept responsibility for our actions within these areas of competence, acknowledging that, even in our areas of strength, there are factors beyond our control.

In the context of AI and according to Raz's view, the concept of responsibility gaps becomes particularly pertinent. Raz's theory can highlight that, as AI systems take over tasks within our 'domains of secure competence', like driving or medical diagnostics, there emerges a challenge in maintaining a clear sense of responsibility and self-conception. If an AI system, operating in a domain traditionally under human mastery, causes an unexpected outcome, it raises the question of who is responsible – the machine, its programmers or the users. Building on Raz, one could argue that this diffusion of responsibility could lead to a disconnection between actions and self-conception. As AI systems increasingly perform tasks that were once direct expressions of our competences, individuals might experience a shift in their understanding of their agency and sense of self. This shift could negatively affect our conceptions of ourselves and disrupt a consistent framework of understanding our own agency, autonomy and place in the world.

A similar train of thought was presented by Wolf, who equally argued that responsibility is intrinsically linked to our status as agents. As mentioned in Part I of this book, Wolf claimed that there is value in

> expressing our recognition that we are beings who are thoroughly in-the-world, in interaction with others whose movements and thoughts we cannot fully control, and whom we affect and are affected by accidentally as well as intentionally, involuntarily, unwittingly, inescapably, as well as voluntarily and deliberately. (Wolf 2001, 14)

Wolf suggests that expressing this recognition and acknowledging our place as agents in the world requires not only our acceptance that harm stemmed from our action, eg driving a lorry, but also our acceptance of responsibility for it. Otherwise, the situation clashes with a proper understanding of ourselves as persons who are in-the-world and also 'defines an approach to life that is unhealthy and undesirable' (Wolf 2001, 13). Thus, from this perspective too, a loss of responsibility would mean a loss, namely a distortion of our self-conception as agents in the world.[3]

A final noteworthy account comes from Tony Honoré. Honoré's view on the significance of responsibility centres around the concept of 'outcome responsibility', which he considers the most fundamental form of responsibility in any society. He argues that outcome responsibility is more essential than moral responsibility, which typically requires fault (in Honoré's understanding), and legal responsibility, which requires either fault or the presence of a special danger. In his view, every decision and action we take is akin to placing a bet on our skills and judgment, making us inherently responsible for the outcomes of our choices. In his words:

> Our responsibility for what we do and for its outcome is inseparable from our status as persons. We cannot disclaim outcome responsibility without undermining that status; and outcome responsibility is therefore more fundamental than moral and legal responsibility, which are species of it. But the fairness of holding someone responsible outside or inside the law depends on their possessing a general capacity for decision and action such that, under the system of bets into which society forces them, they stand over a span of time to win more than they lose .... To bear the risk of bad luck is inseparable from being a choosing person.' (Honoré 1999, 40)

Honoré proposes two main arguments for outcome responsibility. First, it can be seen as fair, under certain conditions, insofar as its allocation of responsibility based on outcomes follows the demand for the fair distribution of benefits and burdens. The fairness of holding someone responsible, either within or outside the law, depends on their general capacity for decision and action. This view implies that living as a choosing individual inherently involves bearing the risk of bad luck, which is an inescapable aspect of human existence and agency. Second, outcome responsibility is crucial to our identity as persons, suggesting that our personhood is defined in part by our ability to make decisions and accept the consequences. Therefore, disclaiming this responsibility would undermine our personhood.

Overall, Honoré, Raz and Wolf all view responsibility as integral to our agency, recognising its significance to how we understand and fill our roles in the world. However, their focal points differ: Honoré emphasises the importance of outcome responsibility and its intrinsic connection to personhood; Raz links responsibility to our 'domains of secure competence', highlighting

[3] For further views on the connection between responsibility and self, see Enoch (2012).

how it shapes our evolving self-conception within our areas of mastery; Wolf, in contrast, focuses on the prudential and aretaic values of responsibility, underscoring its role in fostering a healthy and virtuous approach to life and our interconnectedness with others. But even if each author highlights a different aspect of responsibility – Honoré personhood, Raz self-conception, and Wolf virtue – they collectively affirm the significance of responsibility as a defining element of our agency. Thus, their perspectives explain how the loss of responsibility, particularly in contexts like AI where traditional notions of agency and mastery are challenged, could lead to a disconnection from our sense of self and agency.

Taking Stock

In summary, from the perspective of those bearing responsibility, there are indeed pro-tanto reasons to welcome the absence of responsibility, such as a reduction in psychological costs and other forms of burdens. Nevertheless, even those who bear responsibility will have reason to appreciate the value of embracing it in terms of its significance to morality, our relations to others, and our status as agents, or persons, in the world. Moreover, the standpoint of the patients of responsibility, ie those impacted have a legitimate claim to the accountability of others, is important too, especially when it comes to ensuring justice and maintaining trust. Hence, overall, we can identify some reasons that would favour the creation of responsibility gaps and several considerations that speak against allowing for such gaps. For the purposes of this book, dismissing any arguments in favour of responsibility gaps outright is unnecessary. Rather, it is sufficient to identify reasons to be concerned about these gaps. I take this to be unquestionable, and I believe Danaher would agree. His work is consistent with the view that while there might be immediate advantages to diminishing direct responsibility, the wider implications for moral and social frameworks, as well as for our individual self-conception, deserve thorough contemplation. I therefore conclude that we currently lack an argument as to why we should not be concerned with responsibility gaps. On the contrary, it seems that they can be highly problematic.

In the context of this discussion, however, it is notable that the critique against the need for responsibility becomes most potent when we shift our focus from general answerability to the specific concept of blame. Blame can incur the greatest psychological costs and constitute the greatest burden, while answerability creates a much lower burden. Moreover, answerability suffices to uphold the values of responsibility, eg in terms of a moral conversation that defends moral commitments, in terms of relationship-related accountability practices, and also in terms of maintaining a sense of our own masteries and limitations. I therefore conclude that the responsibility gap is more problematic when it threatens to eliminate answerability.

THE THEORETICAL PROBLEM OF A LACK OF RESPONSIBILITY IN AI

I shall now provide another additional argument as to why responsibility gaps are problematic. I shall argue, not that responsibility gaps are a *practical* problem, ie that they lead to (morally) bad or in some way deplorable situations, but rather that they are also a *theoretical* problem, ie that they create inconsistency in our conceptual frameworks. More precisely, I am going to present a three-step argument to the conclusion that our status as moral agents in the development and use of AI precludes the existence of genuine responsibility gaps. Thus, if our best theories about moral responsibility suggest that there are such gaps, these theories require revision, or otherwise we face contradiction.

But before I proceed, a clarification is in order. In what follows, I shall only focus on moral responsibility as *answerability*, as opposed to moral responsibility in terms of worthiness of blame or praise. I shall here again follow the canonical understanding of answerability as presented, for instance, by Angela Smith, who says: 'a morally responsible [ie answerable] agent is one who can intelligibly be asked to "answer for" her attitudes and conduct' (Angela Smith 2015, 103), where 'to answer for' means 'to give her (justificatory) reasons for thinking, feeling, or acting in the way she has' (Angela Smith 2015, 103). So understood, morally answering for something requires, not just a purely non-rational causal explanation of one's conduct, but an explanation of one's motivation behind one's action and the good one saw in conducting oneself as one did. Moreover, an answerable agent is not yet worthy of blame or praise. Blame or praise will be determined by the kind of explanation a person can provide, eg whether they have an excuse or justification for their conduct.

This focus on answerability limits the scope of my argument to gaps in responsibility-as-answerability and, as a result, I will not be able to directly address responsibility gaps which primarily focus on the attribution of blame and are sometimes described as 'retribution gaps' (Danaher 2016). Nevertheless, the focus on answerability is crucial. If we manage to avoid answerability gaps, we may not have any reason to worry about 'retribution gaps' any more, as I already indicated at the end of chapter six.

(1) We are *Moral Agents* in the Development and Use of AI

Let me start from what I think is a '*given*', something that, I argue, we cannot plausibly deny, namely our moral agency in the development and use of AI. By moral agents, I mean two things: first, when developing and using AI, we are *agents* because we do something, make choices, and thereby *act* rather than being acted upon. Moreover, when using and developing AI, we are *moral* agents because we are guided by values, make normative judgements, and know that our decisions will be morally significant, eg by affecting people's lives in significant ways. Thus, our relation to the effects of AI is fundamentally different from our relation to, say, earthquakes: with regards to the use of AI, we are *moral agents*, whereas with regards to earthquakes, we are *mere patients* (where 'patients' is not a medical term but, in the literal sense, refers to those who are *acted upon* or *suffer* some change, rather than *act* or *cause* change). In fact, it would seem rather implausible to deny our moral agency in the development and use of AI in the way I explained. AI is a human-created technology, and therefore, we cannot think of our relation to the outcomes of AI as we think of our relation to the outcomes of earthquakes.

At this point, I do not intend to make any controversial claim, but rather only confirm our status as moral agents as something that I take to be a very widely shared assumption. The only slightly novel aspect, if there is any, is the view that we can think of our status as moral agents in a domain-specific way: regarding the domain of our deliberate decisions and actions, we are *moral agents* (since we are active in these respects), whereas in the domain of suffering from natural events such as earthquakes, we are *patients* (since we are passive in those respects). However, the substantial parts of my argument start to arise from premise (2) onwards.

(2) Moral *Agency* Requires Moral *Responsibility*

Eshelman claims that 'a moral agent [is] one who qualifies generally as an agent open to responsibility ascriptions'. Parthemore and Whitby agree, when they say: 'By "moral agent", we mean any agent that is appropriately held responsible for its actions' (Parthemore and Whitby 2013, 1). But why is there this connection between moral agency and moral responsibility?

To begin with, it is often considered a fundamental *conceptual* truth that moral agency requires moral responsibility, as in the following statement from Kenneth Himma: 'the idea of moral agency … is *conceptually associated* with the idea of being accountable' (Himma 2009, 21), which – Himma explains – means being responsible.

Moreover, one can further support the view that moral agency requires moral responsibility by highlighting the correlation between a lack of moral responsibility and a lack of moral agency. For instance, children, animals and certain people who lack mental capacity are not (fully) morally responsible and, *for this reason, and to this extent*, also not considered (full) *moral agents* (which, of course, is consistent with their status as beings to whom we owe a certain treatment and who possess rights).

In addition, scholars supported the view that moral agency requires moral responsibility by pointing out that moral agency relies on the existence of deontic categories like 'ought'-statements, obligations, and permissions, and added that such deontic categories could not survive without moral responsibility. As Wolf explained:

> [G]iving up thinking in terms of the notions of responsibility … would require in turn that we … stop thinking in terms of what ought and ought not to be. We would have to stop thinking in terms that would allow the possibility that some lives and projects are better than others. Were we to make ourselves into the kind of creatures that ceased to think in these terms, we would lose the distinction between desires and values and, therefore, our distinction as valuing creatures. (Wolf 1981, 400)[4]

Finally, Stephen Darwall argued that 'the very concept of [a] moral agent … [is] irreducibly second-personal' (Darwall 2010, 219), by which he means, among other things, that moral agency 'implies' (2010, 218) 'being accountable (to someone with the requisite authority) for complying' (2010, 218). In Darwall's view, the very ideas of something being morally right or wrong, as well as something being morally obligatory or prohibited, which are constitutive of moral agency, depend on people being accountable or answerable to each other as moral equals (Darwall 2006).

To support my argument in this section, I rely on such widespread support for the view that moral agency requires moral responsibility. But I also need to emphasise two specifications. First, I will continue to use 'moral agency' in a domain-specific sense, and now add responsibility as a further consideration: I will assume that we possess moral agency in those, and only those, areas in which there is also moral responsibility. We are moral agents with regards to our normal deliberate choices and actions, insofar as we can be morally responsible for them, but we are not moral agents with regards to earthquakes, insofar as we cannot be morally responsible for them. Second, as mentioned before, I will understand moral responsibility in terms of answerability, rather than in terms of liability to praise or blame.

Due to this specification, ie that moral agency requires moral *answerability*, my view can also remain neutral towards the distinct view, rejected by Derk Pereboom (2001) and others (B Waller 2004, 2011; eg Smilansky 1994), according to which moral agency requires moral *liability to praise or blame*. Pereboom defines moral agency in terms of 'powers of reflective self-control – the power to grasp and apply moral reasons, and the power to control or regulate one's behavior by the light of such reasons' (Pereboom 2001, 139). Moral responsibility, on the other hand, is about 'deserv[ing] to be blamed … [or] praised' (Pereboom 2001, 127). On this basis, Pereboom then concludes that there can be moral agency without moral responsibility:

> If hard incompatibilism is true [viz. if determinism precludes moral responsibility], then agents are not morally responsible [i.e. do not deserve praise or blame] for setting ends and choosing means, for formulating principles and making commitments to

[4] See also Van Inwagen (1983, 206–208) and Murphy (1988, 102). Discussion of related aspects in Slote (1990), Vilhauer (2008) and Trakakis (2007).

> them. Nevertheless, the capacities for these activities [and our moral agency] can remain intact. (Pereboom 2001, 151)

I do not need to take a stance on this view. It is consistent to hold, as Pereboom does, that moral agency does *not* require liability to (or worthiness of) praise or blame, *and* also claim, as I do, that moral agency requires *answerability*. In fact, Pereboom himself seems to support this combination of views. He argues that, despite hard incompatibilism and the lack of moral liability to praise or blame, it can still

> be demanded of agents to explain how their decisions accord with the moral reasons, and to consider what their decisions reveal about their moral character and dispositions. The legitimacy of making such demands might be grounded in their value for generating moral improvement … [in this] this sort of moral accountability. (Pereboom 2001, 139)

This type of accountability, or answerability as I would call it, is all that I require for my argument.

However, my proposal opposes a view defended by Luciano Floridi and Jeff Sanders. Floridi and Sanders claim that robots can possess certain abilities constitutive of moral agency, such as interactivity, autonomy, and adaptability, and perform 'morally qualifiable action' (Floridi and Sanders 2004, 364), ie 'action [which] can cause moral good or evil' (Floridi and Sanders 2004, 364).[5] Yet, robots still 'lack a psychological component' (Floridi and Sanders 2004, 367), including consciousness and sentience, which is necessary for moral responsibility. Therefore, Floridi and Sanders conclude, there can be a 'moral agent not necessarily exhibiting … [moral] responsibility' (Floridi and Sanders 2004, 349).

Like Pereboom, Floridi and Sanders focus on responsibility in terms of liability to 'praise and blame' (Floridi and Sanders 2004, 367) and, therefore, my previous reply to Pereboom applies to Floridi and Sanders too. Yet, we may extend Floridi and Sanders's view further and add that robots are not only unable to become morally *liable* to praise or blame, but also unable to become morally *answerable*. Insofar as robots lack certain psychological components, we cannot genuinely hold them morally answerable in the way we hold humans answerable. If anything, we may only demand some kind of error report of the robot's involvement in a harmful chain of events.

But I argue that that Floridi and Sanders fail to show that robots do in fact have moral agency. They only show that robots possess sophisticated abilities to cause changes in their environment, ie *causal* agency, where such changes can be highly morally significant, eg because they harm or even kill people. In Floridi and Sanders's words, such changes are 'morally qualifiable' (Floridi and

[5] On robotic moral agency, see also Moor (2006) and DeBaets (2014).

Sanders 2004, 364). Yet, this does not constitute *moral* agency. Thus, Floridi and Sanders do not present a counterexample to my proposed view after all.

Thus, my view that moral agency requires responsibility as answerability is consistent with the account Pereboom defend, but it opposes the account Floridi and Sanders present.

(3) Hence, Responsibility Gaps in AI cannot Exist

So far, I have argued that (1) we are moral agents in the development and use of AI, and also (2) that moral agency requires moral responsibility (as answerability). Thus, whenever there is moral agency, there must be moral responsibility. So, if we cannot plausibly deny our moral agency in the use and development of AI (as I suggested), we also cannot – as a matter of consistency – lack responsibility. Hence, and this is my conclusion (3): on the assumption of moral agency in the context of AI, genuine responsibility gaps cannot exist. For this reason, the challenge around responsibility gaps (in terms of answerability) can be conceived of, not only as a *practical* problem, leading to undesirable consequences in the world, but also as a *theoretical* problem, namely the problem that the assumption of responsibility gaps would create inconsistency in our conceptual framework.

Before I conclude, however, let me consider an objection to my conclusion. One might argue that we can remain moral agents in the development and use of AI because, *in most cases*, we remain responsible for the consequences of AI. It is just that, *sometimes*, responsibility is lacking due to extraordinary circumstances. But these extraordinary circumstances are not important enough to challenge our status as moral agents.

I agree with a core assumption in this objection: it is certainly correct that even if *some* responsibility gaps exist, we do not lose our moral agency in the development and use of AI *altogether*. Those cases with responsibility gaps leave untouched our moral agency in all other cases, where such gaps to do not arise. I do not intend to claim otherwise, and my argument only focus on cases where responsibility gaps allegedly arise.

But from here, the objection has two flaws. First, it neglects that the situation of potential responsibility gaps become increasingly common, given the fast pace at which AI systems develop and become more 'autonomous' as well as further disconnected from human control and oversight (London 2019; Kiener 2021). Thus, cases of potential responsibility gaps will cease to be the exception and may well become the norm. As a result, the objection becomes hostage to empirical facts which are likely to be false.

Second, even if responsibility gaps are the exception, my conclusion still holds. *When* there are responsibility gaps, there is no way to assert our moral agency any more. We cannot assert moral agency in these cases simply by pointing out that we can assert moral agency in other cases. Doing so would commit an error akin to, but not quite identical to, a fallacy of composition, namely the erroneous inference that something which is true of *most* instances must also be true of *all* instances.

For these two reasons, I argue, the objection ultimately fails and my conclusion that responsibility gaps conflict with the assumption of our moral agency still holds.

CONCLUSION

This chapter addressed the question of why we should be concerned about the absence of moral responsibility in the context of AI. I have built upon the insights provided by Königs, who plausibly debunked some reasons why responsibility gaps are problematic, and Danaher, who highlighted how responsibility gaps might even have positive value for us. I acknowledged the insights of these views but also stated that they exhibit an agent-bias (overlooking the patients of responsibility) and a negativity bias (neglecting the value of moral responsibility for morality, social relationships, and our self-conception). I thus concluded that these accounts cannot, and in fact, did not intend to, argue that responsibility gaps are not a matter of concern. I then formulated an additional theoretical argument leading to the conclusion that responsibility gaps in AI might even be an inconsistent proposition. Therefore, there are both practical and theoretical reasons to be concerned about responsibility gaps. This makes finding a solution to them, and to the *Autonomous AI Conundrum*, urgent.

10

The ABC of Responsible AI

In Part II of this book, I have found that strict moral answerability creates an abundance of responsibility in the context of AI, that there is a normative power of taking responsibility that applies to the use of AI, and that moral responsibility has significant value, such that one cannot deny responsibility gaps by denying the need for responsibility.

In this chapter, I shall bring these insights together and synthesise them into a practical proposal on how we can deal with moral responsibility in the context of AI. I shall take as the starting point the dilemma that the application of strict answerability created, ie the shift from a responsibility gap to responsibility abundance. To recall: an abundance of responsibility is a problem on its own. Once numerous agents are responsible, it becomes impractical to hold all of them responsible. In practice, we simply lack the means to hold everyone answerable and ask them for explanations and justifications for their conduct. But at the same time, we cannot just single some of them out because doing so would be arbitrary and unjust. Therefore, with responsibility abundance there is a dilemma: (i) the great number of agents makes it unfeasible to hold everyone responsible; and (ii) just singling some of them out would be arbitrary or unjust. In other words, it seems that we *cannot* do (i) and we *should not* do (ii). Thus, whereas the problem with a responsibility *gap* is that we lack what we want, the problem with responsibility *abundance* is that we cannot use what we have.

For this reason, dealing with the challenge of responsibility in AI requires an answer to this dilemma. In what follows, I suggest a scheme I call *The ABC of Responsible AI*, which focuses on responsibility practices, combines the ideas of strict moral answerability and the normative power of taking responsibility, and supplements this approach with insights from the ethics and regulation of clinical trials.[1] As in Part I of this book, this will be a *strictness first* approach because I am starting again from the idea of strict moral answerability. However, this time, the normative power of taking responsibility will also play a crucial role and help us deal with the challenges that strict moral answerability creates in the context of AI. *The ABC of Responsible AI* is best understood not as a

[1] I first hinted at this idea in a blog for the Oxford Uehiro Institute: blog.practicalethics.ox.ac.uk/2022/03/the-abc-of-responsible-ai/.

fixed or already fully comprehensive solution, but rather as a general framework on how we ought to deal with responsibility in practical contexts of AI. The letters 'ABC' stand for answerability, blame, and compensation.

ANSWERABILITY

'A' stands for answerability; this builds on the idea of strict moral answerability in particular, and proposes a social practice of responsibility with four key elements.

First, it is essential to establish effective mechanisms for (strict) answerability. A primary barrier to implementing answerability in AI use is that victims often find themselves isolated and powerless against the myriad, more influential agents who caused the harm. To redress this imbalance, the increase in the number of agents causing harm should be matched by an increase in the power of the victims, or patients, who suffered harm. For example, following a serious accident involving an autonomous car, establishing effective mechanisms for answerability may include setting up a dedicated committee or entity that could be mandated to equip victims with the necessary resources to hold responsible parties answerable. This committee could represent various stakeholders, including programmers, manufacturers, regulators and users, in order to facilitate just answerability practices. Current legal solutions sometimes struggle as they tend to be too feeble to effect change, too blunt to address the complexities of individual cases, and, arguably, too confrontational to foster the necessary practice of answerability and mutual conversation.

Second, we will need to specify in advance *what* the different agents must answer for and explain, and this will require spelling out their specific prospective obligations. There are two types of obligations. The first type of obligation concerns the actions and precautions to be taken in AI development and use. These obligations are intimately linked to the role responsibilities of individuals and need to be clearly delineated and established as prerequisites for the technology's legitimate usage, including a comprehensive and explicit protocol. For example, obligations may include that programmers must implement system redundancies and conduct audits, users must operate an AI system only under licensed circumstances, etc. The second type of obligation requires that people not only act in certain ways (when developing or using AI) but also that they provide evidence of their conduct. For instance, manufacturers need to furnish proof of their auditing processes. Such obligations are likely to arise when it is feasible to collect evidence of one's due diligence through the exercise of due diligence itself, but more difficult to uphold when evidence about one's own conduct is hard to provide. But in any case, engaging in risky conduct, which includes the utilisation of high-performing AI systems, requires that we not only take precautions but also prepare ourselves to be able to reassure our fellow citizens of such precautions when challenged to do so. Taken together, these two types of obligations determine who is answerable and for what they are answerable.

Third, we need to distinguish between answerability and explainability. In fact, answerability does not necessarily require the explainability of AI. Individuals can be held answerable for outcomes generated by 'black box' or entirely opaque AI systems for two primary reasons. Firstly, the crux of answerability lies in how individuals fulfil their obligations, which goes beyond understanding the specific causal mechanisms linking the AI system to the resultant harm. Secondly, and as already outlined in chapter two, answerability extends beyond merely providing information. An answerable individual is not akin to an eyewitness whose primary value lies in elucidating events. Rather, such individuals are expected to offer what philosophers sometimes refer to as assurance, second-personal address, and confirmation of their adherence to shared values. This implies that despite their involvement in causing harm, they do not intend to wrong, insult or offend others. This type of assurance is both feasible and necessary, irrespective of the opacity of AI. It is noteworthy that this view, ie that answerability does not depend on explainability or the capacity to elucidate events in detail, is also evident in non-technological contexts. For example, when an individual reacts violently due to an emotional outburst, perhaps after being provoked, and admits to not understanding their own actions, this lack of self-awareness does not exempt them from responsibility. Accordingly, a proper practice of answerability must differentiate between answerability and explainability.

Finally, we need to integrate the normative power of taking responsibility. In some cases where AI leads to a proliferation of strict answerability, or in cases of indeterminacy or even absence of answerability, the previously mentioned points could still be an insufficient remedy. The normative power of taking responsibility can help here and allow us to identify primary addressees of responsibility, encompassing both prospective and retrospective answerability, as outlined in chapters three and eight. Two scenarios are especially noteworthy. In the first scenario, the abundance of strict answerability cannot be sufficiently managed by other means and requires that we employ the normative power of taking responsibility to ensure just and feasible answerability practices. Here, strict moral answerability is already a background consideration, such that responsibility does not need to be conjured from nothing. 'Taking responsibility' would simply mean offering oneself to others as an answerable party and relinquishing one's complaint that being singled out as the answerable party would be arbitrary or unjust. While this approach departs from the more radical nature of the normative power of taking responsibility, as I initially explored, it also guards against one of the most significant objections to this concept, namely the alleged impossibility of creating responsibility *ex nihilo*. The second scenario concerns cases of harm outside the scope of strict answerability (eg cases similar to Thomson's *Day's End*), where it would nevertheless be beneficial to have a practice of answerability. Here, the normative power of taking responsibility would be most radical, as it is indeed about creating responsibility at will. It would make people responsible when they would otherwise not be responsible. My proposed scheme of responsibility practices can feature both kinds of 'taking responsibility'. In addition, it also attends to degrees of moral discretion. Sometimes, people may be obliged to take responsibility in either sense and, sometimes, it may be fully optional. However, in any case, the normative power of taking responsibility must allow for enough moral discretion so that the problem of the power-duty nexus, as explored in chapter three, will not undermine the value of this normative power as a whole.

BLAME

'B' stands for blame and concerns the conditions under which answerable people become liable to blame. This is important because answerability has a link to the liability to blame: an answerable person is presumptively liable to blame, ie they become liable to blame unless they can avert liability with a justification, excuse or other exculpating explanation. Thus, it needs to be stated in advance what standards the multiple agents ought to live up to avert liability to blame.

This ties in with the two types of obligations previously discussed. We must delineate the level of precaution required in an individual's conduct to avoid blame, and assess how a person's causal role in causing harm correlates with the nature and extent of potential blame. Blame, in contrast to answerability, admits of degrees and should reflect the extent of an individual's contribution. Therefore, just as we have defined what a person must answer for, we also need to clarify the scope and magnitude of blame that is appropriate and fitting for them.

Moreover, we need to clarify whether failing to provide evidence alone could make people liable to moral blame, in cases where the actual moral quality of their conduct is unclear. This poses a challenge, as blame is only appropriate for faulty, or culpable, conduct. As Fricker succinctly states: 'No fault, no blame' (Fricker 2016, 170). However, I propose that a responsibility practice might effectively utilise what I term a 'practical presumption of fault'. If certain agents culpably neglect to furnish evidence regarding their conduct when obligated to do so, then their fellow citizens are justifiably entitled to presume fault on their part and consider them liable for blame. This aspect of my proposed responsibility framework seeks to offer a practice-oriented approach, rather than a theoretical resolution of objective moral truths. The concept of presumption, while originating in law, also holds moral legitimacy. (For a discussion of the presumption of fault, see Duff (2009a).)

Clear standards for attributing blame are essential in pinpointing those individuals who are not only answerable but also blameworthy. This helps victims identify the appropriate party to address. In this sense, these standards justify singling out certain agents, making responsibility practices manageable and fair, and avoiding arbitrary decisions. Therefore, clear criteria for blame play a crucial role in enhancing the feasibility and practicality of responsibility practices. Regarding this aspect, however, my proposal maintains neutrality concerning the precise nature of blame, its standards, and its ultimate value. This neutrality is beneficial as it allows my proposal to be adaptable to various theoretical perspectives during implementation. However, my proposal also introduces a novel approach by utilising blame standards to streamline responsibility practices. By employing blame in this manner, we can effectively reduce the number of responsible agents to a more select group, who are especially suited to be the appropriate recipients of such responsibility.

This framework of blame can inform a framework of legal liability too and cover both liability to conviction or punishment (criminal liability) and liability to pay compensation (tort liability). Criminal liability typically requires culpable wrongdoing, while tort liability does not and rather focuses on providing financial compensation for harm caused, irrespective of the actor's moral blameworthiness. When allocating legal liabilities, consideration around blameworthiness can help ensure that financial and criminal consequences are assigned more justly and appropriately. For instance, in cases of criminal liability, considerations about blame can help establish not only whether an individual committed a wrongful act but also whether she did so with a level of moral culpability that warrants punishment. In the realm of tort liability, the primary aim may be to compensate victims, but incorporating considerations about blame can still inform our moral evaluation. For example, when determining the extent of financial compensation or punitive damages, the degree of blameworthiness can influence the final decision, ensuring that those who act with greater moral fault bear a proportionately higher burden.

COMPENSATION

Finally, 'C' signifies compensation, specifically fault-free compensation. This aspect is crucial, as numerous situations may arise where many individuals are answerable, yet none are necessarily to blame or required to offer financial compensation. The presence of strict answerability does not inherently influence or determine the need for compensation, and this represents a significant challenge. But I suggest that AI ethics could here benefit from adopting principles from clinical research ethics, particularly the implementation of a no-fault compensation scheme. Prior to deploying high-risk AI systems, there should be mechanisms in place to compensate victims of harm, irrespective of fault attribution or responsibility assessments. This approach is well-established in clinical research, especially in the realms of experimental treatments and drug trials, where harm can also occur without fault (*cf* McCradden, Stephenson, and Anderson 2020; Holm, Stanton and Bartlett 2021).

By way of background, clinical trials aim to explore new drugs or medical interventions, enrolling human participants to test these developments. Nevertheless, due to inherent uncertainties in research, it is impossible to foresee all potential risks, and sometimes participants are harmed despite the investigators' utmost efforts and diligence. For example, in the 1990s, a trial was conducted during an attempt to develop a drug to treat Hepatitis B. Ex ante, the trial was fully justified, meeting all ethical and scientific standards. An ex post investigation also affirmed the trial's ethical soundness, concluding that 'the entire series of trials reviewed was an ethically sound clinical research project designed and carried out by highly competent investigators who frequently went beyond the requirements dictated by regulations or imposed by IRBs [Institutional Review Boards] to respond to the desires and needs of their patient-subjects' (Institute of Medicine 1995, 10). However, the trial was marred by severe complications, resulting in significant harm to participants' health and, tragically, the deaths of several individuals (Straus 2012).

In such trials, it is essential to include a no-fault compensation scheme. This ensures that before the trial begins, it is established that participants (and/or their families) will receive additional care and compensation if harm is caused during the trial, regardless of whether the harm was due to any fault of the investigators (Childress 1976; Avilés 2014). The situation is similar when using sophisticated AI systems. There is a risk of causing harm without fault, and this calls for a no-fault compensation scheme in the realm of AI too.

This third component is also crucial because the benefits and drawbacks of using new technologies are not naturally distributed equally. Thus, it is important to ensure that in scenarios where an abundance of responsibility complicates compensation, clear guidelines are established. There could be a fund to which all agents involved in the development of AI (who financially benefit from it) contribute. The contributors to this fund would depend on what constitutes a just distribution of benefits and burdens and, thus, this is where responsibility intersects with considerations of justice. When such a scheme of compensation is combined with meaningful practices of answerability, and when there is no culpable conduct, we lose the need for further blaming practices and the worry about 'retribution gaps' becomes unfounded: there may still be an absence of blame and retribution in such cases of harm, but there is no longer any morally justified need for such blame and retribution either.

By way of further clarification: I still think that relying solely on insurance overlooks the distinctive benefits that a responsibility-oriented system provides (see also chapter nine). This is because insurances, while certainly valuable, primarily address the financial aspects of harm and do not cover the broader ethical and moral dimensions of responsibility. For this reason, using insurance as a substitute for responsibility would be inadequate. However, insurance can be an additional component. More specifically: in addition to a responsibility-oriented system, I propose assigning a complementary role to insurance. Insurance can provide necessary financial support and compensation for victims. These are important to create a setting in which victims are not left without recourse or have to wait for a long time when they suffer harm. However, insurances should also be only a part within the broader context of a responsibility framework, so that they support but not replace the moral obligations of individuals and other entities.

So understood, *The ABC of Responsible AI* incorporates the key ideas of this book and translates them into a feasible scheme for the practice and governance of AI. As I shall argue in the next and final chapter, this is not intended to mark the end of the discussion but rather to serve as a starting point – particularly for a broader debate on sustainable AI.

Conclusion

IN THIS BOOK, I introduced a novel philosophical puzzle, the *Lorry Driver Paradox*: a set of three claims that are individually plausible but jointly inconsistent. I used this puzzle to deepen our understanding of moral responsibility and to move beyond two dominant paradigms in the field: the *Reflection View* and *Historicism*. To recap, the *Reflection View* holds that moral answerability, understood as a form of moral responsibility, requires that what one is responsible for reflect the agent's judgement or evaluative stances, while *Historicism* posits that responsibility is grounded solely in the facts about how an action or outcome came about and cannot be altered retrospectively.

The central idea of this book, *strict moral answerability*, resolved the *Lorry Driver Paradox* by challenging the *Reflection View*, while also laying the foundation for the normative power of taking responsibility, thereby challenging *Historicism*. This approach resulted in a new way of thinking about responsibility – one that redefined both the conditions and the scope of responsibility. It transformed responsibility from a primarily intra-personal concept, focused on internal control or the reflection of quality of will, into an interpersonal concept, centred on what we can demand from each other when engaging in risky activities.

Significant parts of this argument were made possible by drawing on ideas from legal scholarship, particularly considerations about reverse burdens of proof in criminal law and the waiving of state immunity in public international law. For this reason, the book also pursued a methodological agenda, advocating for closer integration of legal and philosophical scholarship on the topic of responsibility.

In the second half of the book, I applied these ideas to the context of artificial intelligence, proposing a major shift in thinking about responsibility – namely, moving from the notion of responsibility gaps to that of responsibility abundance, which I argued is an implication of strict moral answerability. I contended that this reframing offers distinctive dialectical and theoretical advantages, allowing us to get a better grip on the challenges AI poses. This perspective also opened up new possibilities for integrating the normative power of taking responsibility and laid the foundation for emphasising the value of responsibility in more specific ways.

Finally, I argued that the core ideas of this book should not only be incorporated into broader conceptual frameworks, whether in philosophy or AI ethics, but also deliver significant practical value. In particular, I introduced my proposed framework, *The ABC of Responsible AI*, to demonstrate how these ideas could inform governance and policy as we deal with further advancements in AI technologies. My aim was to show how these theoretical insights can translate into actionable strategies for addressing the challenges posed by AI.

As I conclude, I wish to emphasise the vital importance of responsibility further by highlighting another increasingly significant consideration: its role in ensuring the *sustainability* of AI. So, rather than signalling the end of the discussion, I shall use the remainder of this final chapter of this book to show that the view presented here can also serve as a foundation for further exploration into the broader ethical and governance challenges that AI presents.

Sustainability, broadly speaking, concerns the question as to how we can meet present needs without compromising the ability of future generations to meet their own. While the concept is commonly associated with environmental and economic dimensions – such as preserving natural resources or ensuring long-term prosperity – it is equally vital to consider *social* sustainability. Social sustainability asks how we can create societal structures that not only satisfy immediate interests today but also assist human flourishing, social cohesion, and peace tomorrow.[1]

It is here that my proposals in this book can play a significant role. Responsibility, understood as a practice of strict moral answerability, facilitates an important conversation between those who caused harm or causally contributed to it and thus can be legitimately held to account, and those who suffered harm and thus have the standing to demand answers. It is a conversation premised on mutual recognition, respect and equality because it asks that people recognise their mutual standpoints, interact with each other as moral equals, show respect for each other's rights and interests, and potentially even make amends when they infringe them. As such, it is a key tool against what we know are the greatest threats to social sustainability, such as discrimination, inequality and polarisation, which new technologies, including AI, are well-known for creating, or at least compounding. Responsibility counteracts discrimination through its commitment to the continuous and mutual recognition of rights and obligations, it challenges inequality by emphasising the fundamental moral equality of individuals when they hold one another answerable to shared moral norms, and it addresses polarisation by fostering a distinctive conversation or dialogue on the reasons, values, and principles that govern conduct. *The ABC of Responsible AI* incorporates these ideals and addresses answerability as a social practice, thereby lending itself very well to developing the means that can support the *socially* sustainable use of AI in practice – something to which, for instance, the predominant responsibility gap theorists have given short shrift. In particular, the combination of two paradigm-shifting ideas from this book, ie strict moral answerability and the

[1] *cf* https://blog.practicalethics.ox.ac.uk/2022/03/the-abc-of-responsible-ai/.

normative power of taking responsibility, together with a range of practical tools, ensure not only that there is responsibility throughout the use of these new technologies but also that such answerability practices can be meaningful, just, and – importantly – also practically feasible.

Thus, the ideas in this book explore new theoretical terrain – ie novel ways in how we think about moral responsibility, how we can link philosophical and legal scholarship, and how to break new theoretical ground in the ethics of AI – and provide new practical perspectives, in particular by addressing the practice of responsibility in ways that promise to render us more capable of *sustainably* availing ourselves of the tremendous benefits that AI may hold for us.

References

Amirfar, Catherine (2019) 'Waivers of Jurisdictional Immunity' in Tom Ruys, Nicolas Angelet and Luca Ferro (eds), *The Cambridge Handbook of Immunities and International Law* (Cambridge, Cambridge University Press) 167–184.

Aristotle (1959) *Politics*, trans H Rackham *Loeb Classical Library 264* (Cambridge, MA, Harvard University Press).

Avilés, Miguel Angel Ramiro (2014) 'Compensation of Research-related Injuries in the European Union' 21 *European Journal of Health Law* 473.

Bathaee, Yavar (2018) 'The Artificial Intelligence Black Box and the Failure of Intent and Causation' 31 *Harvard Journal of Law & Technology* 889.

Baumann, Peter (2021) 'Sorry if! On Conditional Apologies' 24 *Ethical Theory and Moral Practice* 1079.

Bennett, Christopher (2008) *The Apology Ritual: A Philosophical Theory of Punishment* (Cambridge, Cambridge University Press).

—— (2018) 'The Alteration Thesis: Forgiveness as a Normative Power' 46(2) *Philosophy & Public Affairs* 207.

—— (2022) 'What Goes On When We Apologize?' 23 *Journal of Ethics & Social Philosophy* 115.

Bernstein, Sara (2017) 'Causal Proportions and Moral Responsibility' 4 *Oxford Studies in Agency and Responsibility* 165.

Bero, Stephen (2020) 'Holding Responsible and Taking Responsibility' 39 *Law and Philosophy* 263.

Bovens, Luc (2008) 'Apologies' *Proceedings of the Aristotelian Society*.

Braithwaite, John and Philip Pettit (1990) *Not Just Deserts – A Republican Theory of Criminal Justice* (Oxford, Oxford University Press).

Bröhmer, Jürgen (1997) *State Immunity and the Violation of Human Rights* (The Hague, Martinus Nijhoff Publishers).

Capes, Justin A (2019) 'Strict Moral Liability' 36 *Social Philosophy and Policy* 52.

Carpenter, Catherine L (2003) 'On Statutory Rape, Strict Liability, and the Public Welfare Offense Model' 53 *American University Law Review* 313.

Champagne, Marc, and Ryan Tonkens (2015) 'Bridging the Responsibility Gap in Automated Warfare' 28 *Philosophy & Technology* 125.

Chang, Ruth (2020) 'Do We Have Normative Powers?' 94 *Aristotelian Society Supplementary Volume* 275.

Childress, James F (1976) 'Compensating Injured Research Subjects: I. The Moral Argument' *Hastings Center Report* 21.

Coeckelbergh, Mark (2020) 'Artificial Intelligence, Responsibility Attribution, and a Relational Justification of Explainability' 26 *Science and Engineering Ethics* 2051.

Cohen, Marc A (2018) 'Apology as Self-repair' 21 *Ethical Theory and Moral Practice* 585.

Cornford, Andrew (2011) *The Structures of the Criminal Law* (Oxford, Oxford University Press).

Cowley, Christopher (2013) *Moral Responsibility* (Durham, Acumen Publishing).

Crawford, James, and Ian Brownlie (2019) *Brownlie's Principles of Public International Law* 9th edn (Oxford, Oxford University Press).

Cunningham, Michael J (2014) *States of Apology* (Manchester, Manchester University Press).

Danaher, John (2016) 'Robots, Law and the Retribution Gap' 18 *Ethics and Information Technology* 299.

—— (2022) 'Tragic Choices and the Virtue of Techno-Responsibility Gaps' 35 *Philosophy & Technology* 1.
Darwall, Stephen (2006) *The Second-person Standpoint: Morality, Respect, and Accountability* (Cambridge, MA, Harvard University Press).
—— (2010) 'Precis: The Second-person Standpoint' 81 *Philosophy and Phenomenological Research* 216.
Davis, Paul (2002) 'On Apologies' 19 *Journal of Applied Philosophy* 169.
De Jong, Roos (2020) 'The Retribution-Gap and Responsibility-Loci Related to Robots and Automated Technologies: A Reply to Nyholm' 26 *Science and Engineering Ethics* 727.
DeBaets, Amy Michelle (2014) 'Can a Robot Pursue the Good? Exploring Artificial Moral Agency' 24(3) *Journal of Ethics and Emerging Technologies* 76.
Dennis, Ian (2005) 'Reverse Onuses and the Presumption of Innocence: In Search of Principle' *Criminal Law Review* 901.
Denza, Eileen (2016) 'Article 32: Waiver of Immunity' in *Diplomatic Law: Commentary on the Vienna Convention on Diplomatic Relations* 4th edn (Oxford, Oxford University Press).
Difonzo, Nicholas, Anthony Alongi and Paul Wiele (2020) 'Apology, Restitution, and Forgiveness after Psychological Contract Breach' 161(1) *Journal of Business Ethics* 53.
Dubber, Markus D, Frank Pasquale and Sunit Das (2020) *The Oxford Handbook of Ethics of AI* (Oxford, Oxford University Press).
Duff, Antony (2009a) *Answering for Crime: Responsibility and Liability in the Criminal Law* (Oxford, Hart Publishing).
—— (2009b) 'Legal and Moral Responsibility' 4 *Philosophy Compass* 978.
—— (2019) 'Moral and Criminal Responsibility – Answering and Refusing to Answer' in J Coates and N Tognazzini (eds), *Oxford Studies in Agency and Responsibility, Volume 5* (Oxford, Oxford University Press).
—— (2021) 'Criminal Responsibility without Blame?' *Unpublished manuscript.*
Enoch, David (2012) 'Being Responsible, Taking Responsibility, and Penumbral Agency' in Ulrike Heuer and Gerald Lang (eds), *Luck, Value, and Commitment: Themes from the Ethics of Bernard Williams* (Oxford, Oxford University Press) 95–131.
Ficuciello, Fanny, Guglielmo Tamburrini, Alberto Arezzo, Luigi Villani and Bruno Siciliano (2019) 'Autonomy in Surgical Robots and its Meaningful Human Control' 10 *Paladyn: Journal of Behavioral Robotics* 30.
Finke, Jasper (2010) 'Sovereign Immunity: Rule, Comity or Something Else?' 21(4) *European Journal of International Law* 853.
Fischer, John Martin, and Mark Ravizza (1998) *Responsibility and Control: A Theory of Moral Responsibility* (Cambridge, Cambridge University Press).
Floridi, Luciano, and Jeff W Sanders (2004) 'On the Morality of Artificial Agents' 14 *Minds and Machines* 349.
Fox, Hazel, and Philippa Webb (2015) *The Law of State Immunity* 3rd edn (Oxford, Oxford University Press).
Frankfurt, Harry G (1969) 'Alternate Possibilities and Moral Responsibility' 66(23) *The Journal of Philosophy* 829.
—— (1975) 'Three Concepts of Free Action' 49 *Proceedings of the Aristotelian Society, Supplementary Volumes* 95.
Fricker, Miranda (2016) 'What's the Point of Blame? A Paradigm Based Explanation' 50 *Noûs* 165.
Funkhouser, Eric (2009) 'Frankfurt Cases and Overdetermination' 39 *Canadian Journal of Philosophy* 341.
Gamlund, Espen (2010) 'The Duty to Forgive Repentant Wrongdoers' 18 *International Journal of Philosophical Studies* 651.
Gardner, John (2005) 'Wrongs and Faults' in A Simester, *Appraising Strict Liability* (Oxford, Oxford University Press) 51–80.

—— (2011) 'What is Tort Law for? Part 1. The Place of Corrective Justice' 30 *Law and Philosophy* 1.
—— (2018) *From Personal Life to Private Law* (Oxford, Oxford University Press).
Gill, Kathleen (2000) 'The Moral Functions of an Apology' 31 *Philosophical Forum* 11.
Govier, Trudy, and Wilhelm Verwoerd (2002) 'The Promise and Pitfalls of Apology' 33 *Journal of Social Philosophy* 67.
Griswold, Charles L (2007) *Forgiveness: A Philosophical Exploration* (Cambridge, Cambridge University Press).
Gunkel, David J (2017) 'Mind the Gap: Responsible Robotics and the Problem of Responsibility' *Ethics and Information Technology* 1.
Harris, John (2011) 'Moral Enhancement and Freedom' 25 *Bioethics* 102.
Harris, Sandra, Karen Grainger and Louise Mullany (2006) 'The Pragmatics of Political Apologies' 17 *Discourse & Society* 715.
Hart, HLA (1955) 'Are There Any Natural Rights?' 64 *The Philosophical Review* 175.
Hasker, William (2000) 'The Problem of Evil in Process Theism and Classical Free Will Theism' 29 *Process Studies* 194.
Helmreich, Jeffrey S (2015) 'The Apologetic Stance' 43 *Philosophy & Public Affairs* 75.
Herring, Jonathan (2020) *Criminal Law: Text, Cases, and Materials* 9th edn (Oxford, Oxford University Press).
Heuer, Ulrike (2012a) 'Promising – Part 1' 7 *Philosophy Compass* 832.
—— (2012b) 'Promising – Part 2' 7 *Philosophy Compass* 842.
Hieronymi, Pamela (2001) 'Articulating an Uncompromising Forgiveness' 62 *Philosophy and Phenomenological Research* 529.
—— (2004) 'The Force and Fairness of Blame' 18 *Philosophical Perspectives* 115.
Himma, Kenneth Einar (2009) 'Artificial Agency, Consciousness, and the Criteria for Moral Agency: What Properties Must an Artificial Agent Have to Be a Moral Agent?' 11 *Ethics and Information Technology* 19.
Himmelreich, Johannes (2019) 'Responsibility for Killer Robots' 22 *Ethical Theory and Moral Practice* 731.
Hohfeld, Wesley Newcomb (1913) 'Some Fundamental Legal Conceptions as Applied in Judicial Reasoning' 23 *The Yale Law Journal* 16.
Holm, Søren, Catherine Stanton and Benjamin Bartlett (2021) 'A New Argument for No-Fault Compensation in Health Care: The Introduction of Artificial Intelligence Systems' 29 *Health Care Analysis* 171.
Honoré, Tony (1999) *Responsibility and Fault* (Oxford, Hart Publishing).
Hubbs, Graham (2013) 'Answerability without Answers' 7 *Journal of Ethics and Social Philosophy* 1.
Hurd, Heidi M (1996) 'The Moral Magic of Consent' 2 *Legal Theory* 121.
Husak, Douglas (2010) 'Answering Duff: R.A. Duff's Answering for Crime (Book Review)' 29 *Law and Philosophy* 101.
Institute of Medicine (1995) *Review of the Fialuridine (FIAU) Clinical Trials.* Edited by Frederick J Manning and Morton Swartz (Washington, DC The National Academies Press).
Johnson, Deborah G (2015) 'Technology with No Human Responsibility?' 127 *Journal of Business Ethics* 707.
Juratowitch, Ben (2016) 'Waiver of State Immunity and Enforcement of Arbitral Awards' 6 *Asian Journal of International Law* 199.
Kaiserman, Alex (2016) 'Causal Contribution' *Proceedings of the Aristotelian Society.*
—— (2021) 'Responsibility and the "Pie Fallacy"' *Philosophical Studies* 1.

Kamtekar, Rachana, and Shaun Nichols (2019) 'Agent-Regret and Accidental Agency' 43 *Midwest Studies in Philosophy* 181.
Kiener, Maximilian (2021) 'Artificial Intelligence in Medicine and the Disclosure of Risks' 36 *AI & Society* 705.
—— (2022) 'Can We Bridge AI's Responsibility Gap at Will?' 25 *Ethical Theory and Moral Practice* 575.
—— (2023) 'Varieties of Answerability' in Maximilian Kiener (ed), *The Routledge Handbook of Philosophy of Responsibility* (London, Routledge) 204–216.
—— (2024) 'Strict Moral Answerability' 134 *Ethics* 360.
—— (2025) 'AI and Responsibility: No Gap, but Abundance' 42 *Journal of Applied Philosophy* 357.
Kim, Tae (2014) 'Decent Termination: A Moral Case for Severance Pay' 24 *Business Ethics Quarterly* 203.
Königs, Peter (2022) 'Artificial Intelligence and Responsibility Gaps: What is the Problem?' 24 *Ethics and Information Technology* 1.
Kort, Louis F (1975) 'What is an Apology?' 1 *Philosophy Research Archives* 78.
Kramer, Matthew H (2005) 'Moral Rights and the Limits of the Ought-Implies-Can Principle: Why Impeccable Precautions are No Excuse' 48 *Inquiry* 307.
Lazare, Aaron (2004) *On Apology* (New York, Oxford University Press).
Lewinsohn, Jed (2024). 'The "Natural Unintelligibility" of Normative Powers' 15 *Jurisprudence* 5.
Lewis, David (1973) 'Causation' 70 *Journal of Philosophy* 556.
—— (2000) 'Causation as Influence' 97 Journal of Philosophy 182.
List, Christian (2021) 'Group Agency and Artificial Intelligence' 34 *Philosophy & Technology* 1213.
London, AJ (2019) 'Artificial Intelligence and Black-Box Medical Decisions: Accuracy Versus Explainability' 49 *Hastings Center Report* 15.
MacKenzie, Jordan (2017) 'Agent-Regret and the Social Practice of Moral Luck' 94 *Res Philosophica* 95.
MacLachlan, Alice (2018) 'Fiduciary Duties and the Ethics of Public Apology' 35 *Journal of Applied Philosophy* 359.
Mason, Elinor (2018) 'Respecting Each Other and Taking Responsibility for Our Biases' in Katrina Hutchison, Catriona Mackenzie and Marina Oshana (eds), *Social Dimensions of Moral Responsibility* (Oxford, Oxford University Press) 163–184.
—— (2019) *Ways to be Blameworthy: Rightness, Wrongness, and Responsibility* (Oxford, Oxford University Press).
—— (2023) 'Taking Responsibility' in Maximilian Kiener (ed), *The Routledge Handbook of Philosophy of Responsibility* (London, Routledge) 357–367.
Matthias, Andreas (2004) 'The Responsibility Gap: Ascribing Responsibility for the Actions of Learning Automata' 6 *Ethics and Information Technology* 175.
McCradden, Melissa D, Elizabeth A Stephenson and James A Anderson (2020) 'Clinical Research Underlies Ethical Integration of Healthcare Artificial Intelligence' 26 *Nature Medicine* 1325.
McGeer, Victoria (2019) 'Scaffolding Agency: A Proleptic Account of the Reactive Attitudes' 27 *European Journal of Philosophy* 301.
McGeer, Victoria and Philip Pettit (2015) 'The Hard Problem of Responsibility' in D Shoemaker (ed), *Oxford Studies in Agency and Responsibility* (Vol 3) (Oxford, Oxford University Press) 160–188.
Menges, Leonhard (2017) 'The Emotion Account of Blame' 174 *Philosophical Studies* 257.
Milam, Per-Erik (2019) 'Reasons to Forgive' 79 *Analysis* 242.
Miller, Kristie (2014) 'Conditional and Prospective Apologies' 48 *Journal of Value Inquiry* 403.
Milton, John (2014) *Paradise Lost* (Minneapolis, MN: First Avenue Editions).
Montminy, Martin (2019) 'Derivative Culpability' 49 *Canadian Journal of Philosophy* 689.

Moor, JH (2006) 'The Nature, Importance, and Difficulty of Machine Ethics' 21 *IEEE Intelligent Systems* 18.

Munch, Lauritz, Jakob Mainz and Jens Christian Bjerring (2023) 'The Value of Responsibility Gaps in Algorithmic Decision-making' 25 *Ethics and Information Technology* 21.

Murphy, Jeffrie G (1988) 'Hatred: A Qualified Defense' in J Murphy and J Hampton (eds), *Forgiveness and Mercy* (Cambridge, Cambridge University Press) 88–110.

Nagel, Thomas (1979) *Mortal Questions* (Cambridge, Cambridge University Press).

—— (1986) *The View From Nowhere* (Oxford: Oxford University Press).

Nyholm, Sven (2020) *Humans and Robots – Ethics, Agency, and Anthropomorphism* (Rowman & Littlefield Publishers).

Owens, David (2012) *Shaping the Normative Landscape* (Oxford, Oxford University Press).

Parthemore, Joel, and Blay Whitby (2013) 'What Makes Any Agent a Moral Agent? Reflections on Machine Consciousness and Moral Agency' 5 *International Journal of Machine Consciousness* 105.

Pereboom, Derk (2001) *Living Without Free Will* (Cambridge, Cambridge University Press).

Pettit, Philip (1997) *Republicanism: A Theory of Freedom and Government* (Oxford, Oxford University Press).

—— (2005) 'The Domination Complaint' 46 *Nomos* 87.

Piovarchy, Adam (2020) 'Blame in the Aftermath of Excused Wrongdoing' 34 *Public Affairs Quarterly* 142.

Poel, Ibo van de, Lambèr MM Royakkers and Sjoerd D Zwart (2015) *Moral Responsibility and the Problem of Many Hands* (London, Routledge).

Quong, Jonathan (2015) 'Rights against Harm' 89 *Proceedings of the Aristotelian Society, Supplementary Volumes* 249.

Rawls, J (2005) *Political Liberalism* (New York, Columbia University Press).

Raz, Joseph (1986) *The Morality of Freedom* (Oxford, Clarendon Press).

—— (1999) *Practical Reason and Norms* (Oxford, Oxford University Press).

—— (2009) *The Authority of Law: Essays on Law and Morality* 2nd edn (Oxford, Oxford University Press).

—— (2011) *From Normativity to Responsibility* (Oxford, Oxford University Press).

—— (2019) 'Normative Powers' *SSRN Electronic Journal.*

Roberts, Paul, and Adrian Zuckerman (2010) *Criminal Evidence* 2nd edn (Oxford, Oxford University Press).

Robichaud, Philip, and Jan Willem Wieland (2017) *Responsibility: The Epistemic Condition* (Oxford, Oxford University Press).

Santoni de Sio, Filippo, and Ezio Di Nucci (2018) 'Pushing the Margins of Responsibility: Lessons from Parks' Somnambulistic Killing' 11 *Neuroethics* 35.

Santoni de Sio, Filippo, and Giulio Mecacci (2021) 'Four Responsibility Gaps with Artificial Intelligence: Why They Matter and How to Address Them' *Philosophy & Technology* 1.

Sartorio, Carolina (2012) 'Two Wrongs Do Not Make a Right: Responsibility and Overdetermination' 18 *Legal Theory* 473.

Scanlon, TM (2000) *What We Owe to Each Other* (Cambridge, MA, Belknap Press)

—— (2008) *Moral Dimensions: Permissibility, Meaning, Blame* (Cambridge, MA, Belknap Press).

Schiff, D, and J Borenstein (2019) 'How Should Clinicians Communicate With Patients About the Roles of Artificially Intelligent Team Members?' 21 *AMA Journal of Ethics* E138.

Schulzke, Marcus (2013) 'Autonomous Weapons and Distributed Responsibility' 26 *Philosophy & Technology* 203.

Shademan, Azad, Ryan S Decker, Justin D Opfermann, Simon Leonard, Axel Krieger and Peter CW Kim (2016) 'Supervised Autonomous Robotic Soft Tissue Surgery' 8(337) *Science Translational Medicine* 337ra64.

Shiffrin, Seana Valentine (2008) 'Promising, Intimate Relationships, and Conventionalism' 117 *Philosophical Review* 481.
Shoemaker, David (2013) 'On Criminal and Moral Responsibility' in Mark Timmons (ed), *Oxford Studies in Normative Ethics: Vol 3* (Oxford, Oxford University Press) 154–178.
—— (2015) *Responsibility From the Margins* (Oxford: Oxford University Press).
—— (2017) 'Response-dependent Responsibility; or, a Funny Thing Happened on the Way to Blame' 126 *Philosophical Review* 481.
Shoemaker, David, and Manuel Vargas (2021) 'Moral Torch Fishing: A Signaling Theory of Blame' 55 *Noûs* 581.
Shuman, Daniel W (2000) 'The Role of Apology in Tort Law' 83 *Judicature* 180.
Simester, AP (2021) *Fundamentals of Criminal Law: Responsibility, Culpability, and Wrongdoing* (Oxford, Oxford University Press).
Simpson, Thomas W, and Vincent C Müller (2016) 'Just War and Robots' Killings' 66(263) *The Philosophical Quarterly* 302.
Singer, Peter (1972) 'Famine, Affluence, and Morality' *Philosophy & Public Affairs* 229.
Sliwa, Paulina (2019) 'The Power of Excuses' 47 *Philosophy & Public Affairs* 37.
—— (2023) 'Apologies: An Anatomy' *unpublished manuscript.*
Slote, Michael (1990) 'Ethics without Free Will' 16 *Social Theory and Practice* 369.
Smilansky, Saul (1994) 'The Ethical Advantages of Hard Determinism' 54 *Philosophy and Phenomenological Research* 355.
Smith, Adam (2009) *The Theory of Moral Sentiments* (London, Penguin).
Smith, Angela (2005) 'Responsibility for Attitudes: Activity and Passivity in Mental Life' 115 *Ethics* 236.
—— (2015) 'Responsibility as Answerability' 58 *Inquiry* 99.
Smith, Nick (2008) *I Was Wrong: The Meanings of Apologies* (Cambridge, Cambridge University Press).
—— (2014) *Justice Through Apologies: Remorse, Reform, and Punishment* (Cambridge, Cambridge University Press).
Sparrow, Robert (2007) 'Killer Robots' 24 *Journal of Applied Philosophy* 62.
Straus, Stephen (2012) 'Unanticipated Risk in Clinical Research' in John Gallin and Frederick Ognibene (eds), *Principles and Practice of Clinical Research* (London, Elsevier/Academic Press) 109–126.
Strawson, PF (1963) *Freedom and Resentment. Annual philosophical lecture, Henriette Hertz Trust; 1962* (London: The British Academy).
Stumer, Andrew C (2010) *The Presumption of Innocence: Evidential and Human Rights Perspectives (Criminal Law Library 8)* (Oxford, Hart Publishing).
Sussman, David (2018) 'Is Agent-Regret Rational?' 128 *Ethics* 788.
Tadros, Victor (2016) *Wrongs and Crimes* (Oxford, Oxford University Press).
—— (2020a) 'Appropriate Normative Powers' *Aristotelian Society Supplementary Volume.*
—— (2020b) 'Distributing Responsibility' 48 *Philosophy & Public Affairs* 223.
Thomson, Judith Jarvis (1990) *The Realm of Rights* (Cambridge, MA, Harvard University Press).
Tigard, Daniel W (2020) 'There Is No Techno-responsibility Gap' *Philosophy & Technology*: 1.
Trakakis, Nick (2007) 'Whither Morality in a Hard Determinist World?' *Sorites* 19.
Turner, Jacob (2019) *Robot Rules: Regulating Artificial Intelligence* (Palgrave Macmillan).
Van Inwagen, Peter (1983) *An Essay on Free Will* (Oxford, Clarendon Press).
Velleman, James David (2015) *Beyond Price: Essays on Birth and Death* (Cambridge, Open Book Publishers).
Verdier, Pierre-Hugues, and Erik Voeten (2015) 'How Does Customary International Law Change? The Case of State Immunity' 59 *International Studies Quarterly* 209.
Vilhauer, Ben (2008) 'Hard Determinism, Humeanism, and Virtue Ethics' 46 *Southern Journal of Philosophy* 121.

Wallace, R Jay (1994) *Responsibility and the Moral Sentiments* (Cambridge, MA, Harvard University Press).
Waller, Bruce (2004) 'Virtue Unrewarded: Morality Without Moral Responsibility' 31 *Philosophical Quarterly of Israel* 427.
—— (2011) *Against Moral Responsibility* (Cambridge, MA, MIT Press).
Waller, Bruce N (2007) 'Sincere Apology Without Moral Responsibility' 33 *Social Theory and Practice* 441.
Warmke, Brandon (2016) 'The Normative Significance of Forgiveness' 94 *Australasian Journal of Philosophy* 687.
Watson, Gary (1996) 'Two Faces of Responsibility' 24 *Philosophical Topics* 227.
—— (2004) *Agency and Answerability: Selected Essays* (Oxford, Oxford University Press).
—— (2009) 'Promises, Reasons, and Normative Powers' in David Sobel and Steven Wall (eds) *Reasons for Action* (Cambridge, Cambridge University Press) 155–178.
Westlund, Andrea (2013) 'Deference as a Normative Power' 166 *An International Journal for Philosophy in the Analytic Tradition* 455.
Williams, Bernard (1981) *Moral Luck: Philosophical Papers, 1973–1980* (Cambridge, Cambridge University Press).
Wolf, Susan (1981) 'The Importance of Free Will' 90 (359) *Mind* 386.
—— (2001) 'The Moral of Moral Luck' 31 *Philosophic Exchange* 2.
—— (2011) 'Blame, Italian Style' in Rahul Kumar, R Jay Wallace and Samuel Freeman (eds), *Reasons and Recognition: Essays on the Philosophy of T.M. Scanlon* (Oxford, Oxford University Press).
Zimmerman, Michael J (1985) 'Sharing Responsibility' 22 *American Philosophical Quarterly* 115.

Index

www.ingramcontent.com/pod-product-compliance
Ingram Content Group UK Ltd.
Pitfield, Milton Keynes, MK11 3LW, UK
UKHW021311300626
472601UK00007B/83

9 781509 956845